A PLANETARY AWAKENING IN LOVE THROUGH UNIQUE SELF SYMPHONIES

A PLANETARY AWAKENING IN LOVE THROUGH UNIQUE SELF SYMPHONIES

TOWARDS A POLITICS OF EVOLUTIONARY LOVE

CONFESSING YOUR GREATNESS

• • •

From Conscious Evolution 1.0 to Conscious Evolution 2.0

One Mountain, Many Paths: Oral Essays
Volume One

DR. MARC GAFNI AND
BARBARA MARX HUBBARD

Authors: Marc Gafni and Barbara Marx Hubbard
Title: A Planetary Awakening in Love Through Unique Self Symphonies
From Conscious Evolution 1.0 to Conscious Evolution 2.0

Identifiers: ISBN 979-8-88834-044-8 (electronic)
ISBN 979-8-88834-004-2 (paperback)

© 2025 Marc Gafni

Edited by Kristina Amelong

World Philosophy and Religion Press,
in conjunction with

IP Integral Publishers

https://worldphilosophyandreligion.org

JOIN THE REVOLUTION!

CONTENTS

CHAPTER 8   OUTRAGEOUS LOVE IS A PERCEPTION

CHAPTER 9   RECLAIMING GOD AS EVOLUTION: BEYOND
THE EXILE OF EVOLUTION TO TECHNOLOGY

EDITORIAL NOTE ABOUT AUTHORSHIP, EDITING, AND THE RADICAL CONTEXT FOR THIS SERIES

ORAL ESSAYS FROM THE ONE MOUNTAIN, MANY PATHS WEEKLY BROADCAST

This volume is part of the Oral Essays library, a series of lightly edited, compiled transcripts of oral teachings given by Dr. Marc Gafni and the late Barbara Marx Hubbard in their weekly online broadcast, *One Mountain, Many Paths,* which they co-founded in 2017. Originally called an "Evolutionary Church," *One Mountain, Many Paths* became a key venue for the articulation of an inspired and deeply grounded new Story of Value in response to the meta-crisis. Marc and Barbara—together with Zak Stein,[1] Kristina Kincaid, Ken Wilber, Sally Kempton, Lori Galperin, Aubrey Marcus and dozens of other thought-leaders over the years—began to articulate what they call a World Philosophy and World Religion[2] as a context for our diversity.

---

1   Zak, together with Ken Wilber, has been Marc's primary intellectual partner and an initiate lineage holder in CosmoErotic Humanism.

2 This project is grounded in four core organizational frameworks: 1) The Center for World Philosophy and Religion, co-founded by Marc Gafni, Zachary Stein, Sally Kempton, and Ken Wilber, and chaired over the years by John P. Mackey, Barbara Marx Hubbard, Aubrey Marcus, Gabrielle Anwar and Shareef Malnik, Carrie Kish and Adam Bellow, and Kathleen J. Brownback. 2) The Office for the Future, chaired by Stephanie Valcke and Ivan Bossyut. 3) The World Philosophy and Religion Press, founded and chaired by Aubrey Marcus, together with Marc Gafni and Zachary Stein. 4) The Foundation for Conscious Evolution, founded by Barbara Marx Hubbard and currently chaired by Peter Fiekowsky. For a complete list of key leadership, see the Office for the Future website, www.officeforthefuture.com.

Until Barbara's passing in 2019, she and Marc transmitted teachings together as evolutionary partners and "whole mates," weaving together insights and transmissions from their decades of practice, study, teaching, and activism into a synergy of wisdom, a grounded vision for future policy across all sectors of society.

Much of the *dharma* material below comes directly from Marc, so it was originally all in quotation marks—but that looked a little odd. So per his suggestion we removed them, and the reader should consider the paragraphs on the next several pages as one extended quote from him. We are joyfully grateful to Marc for the clarity of his *dharma*, the elegance and "second simplicity" of this language, and the mad, Outrageous Love with which he transmits his teachings.

Barbara and Marc called the mission of *One Mountain* "a Planetary Awakening in Evolutionary Love Through Unique Self Symphonies." We are an evolutionary community with a deeply grounded, radically alive, and "post-tragic" revolutionary spirit. We are activating a new humanity and awakening as a new species: *Homo amor*, the fulfillment of *Homo sapiens*.

One Mountain is committed to articulating a Story of Value that can become the ground for the new society that must be birthed in response to the meta-crisis. We recognize that we are living at a pivotal moment in history. In this "time between stories," the great moral imperative is to tell the new Story of Value. It is ours to do, personally and collectively, with great trembling and ecstatic joy.

FROM DOGMA TO *DHARMA*: ETERNAL AND EVOLVING FIRST PRINCIPLES AND FIRST VALUES

The teachings are grounded in decades of deep study across many wisdom traditions. Over the years, week by week, these teachings were incrementally developed within the framework of the *One Mountain, Many Paths* broadcast. We often refer to these teachings as *dharma*.

This word was originally used in lineage traditions to refer to something like universal law. This is a crucial realization: just as there is universal law in mathematical value, there is also a sense of universal law in ethics and value.

Historically, *dharma* often devolved into unchanging dogma. Evolution was ignored, and the natural process of *dharma* evolution became disconnected from its deep, eternal context. The weakness of the word *dharma* is that too often it did not include the evolving insights of the sciences, it confused local cultural truths with universal truths, and it used words like "eternal," as in "eternal Tao," as opposed to words like "evolution."

Eternal came to mean unchanging, and that kind of thinking often led to overly ethnocentric readings of *dharma*. Local systems would claim their religious and cultural insights as immutable, which stood in the way of the emergence of a genuine world Story of Value that is real, inherent to Cosmos, and backed by the Universe—even as it is also always evolving.

Or, as we often say, "eternal value is evolving value. The eternal Tao is the evolving Tao."

We have shown that, emergent from profound insights in the "interior sciences," eternal does not mean unchanging in time; it means what we call the deeper Field of ErosValue that is beneath culture, geography, and history, which lives beneath all individual and collective values, and beneath time and space itself.

As such, we have gradually transitioned from the term *dharma* to the term *Value*, in the sense of the Field of Value that lives beneath all values. This Field of Value discloses as First Principles and First Values embedded in a Story of Value.

Indeed, as the interior sciences knew and the exterior sciences imply, Reality arises in a Field of ErosValue in which an entire set of mathematical, musical, molecular, moral, and mystical values are the very ground of all being. That Field of Value is eternal—the true ground of the Good, True and Beautiful—even as it is evolving.

But of course, it is equally critical not just to talk about evolving value, but to ground the evolving value in its true nature, the eternal Field of First Principles and First Values, always reaching for ever-more life, ever-more love, ever-more care, ever-more depth, ever-more uniqueness, ever-more intimate communion, and ever-more transformation.

As such, when we refer to the word *dharma*, which still appears in these texts together with the word value, we refer to an evolving *dharma* grounded in an *eternal and evolving* Field of Value. Indeed, eternity and evolution are two faces of the whole, opposites joined at the hip, that characterize the nature of our Cosmos in virtually all of its expressions.

It's in these terms that we ground a robust world philosophy that integrates the validated, leading-edge insights of premodern traditional wisdom, modern wisdom, and more recent postmodern insights, weaving them together into a new whole greater than the sum of its parts.

This new whole is a shared Story of Value rooted in First Principles and First Values that are both eternal and evolving.

These First Principles and First Values of Cosmos are woven together into a new Story of Value as a context for our diversity, a new Universe Story. This new Story gives us the best possible responses we have to the mystery, and to the great questions:

- ◆ Who am I? Who are we?
- ◆ Where am I? Where are we?
- ◆ What should I do? What should we do?

It is only through such a shared Universe Story—a narrative of identity and ethos as a context for our blessed diversity—that we can realize how what unites is so much greater than what divides us.

Only a new Story of Value will allow us to both respond to the meta-crisis and participate together in birthing the most true, good, and beautiful world that we already know is possible.

THIS ORAL ESSAYS SERIES IS AN ENTRYWAY TO THE GREAT LIBRARY OF COSMOEROTIC HUMANISM

This Oral Essays series is part of the overarching project of the Great Library at the Center for World Philosophy and Religion, led by Dr. Marc Gafni, together with Dr. Zak Stein. The aim of the Great Library project is to articulate a robust and comprehensive new Story of Value, CosmoErotic Humanism, in the form of dozens of well-researched and extensively footnoted academic works.

Our vision is to provide the philosophical framework that will be vital for navigating humanity through this time of immense crisis and transformation.

To begin your journey into CosmoErotic Humanism, we tenderly refer you to the book *First Principles and First Values*, co-authored by Marc Gafni, Zak Stein, and Ken Wilber, under the name David J. Temple. David J. Temple is a pseudonym created for enabling ongoing collaborative authorship at the Center for World Philosophy and Religion. The two primary authors behind David J. Temple are Marc Gafni and Zak Stein, and for different projects, specific writers will be named as part of the collaboration, such as Ken Wilber and others.

Three other volumes complete this introduction: *A Return to Eros*, by Marc Gafni and Kristina Kincaid; *Your Unique Self*, by Marc Gafni; and *Education in a Time between Worlds*, by Zak Stein.

We hope that the Oral Essays in this volume, with their informal style of transmission, will serve as an allurement and entryway for you into the more formal books of the Great Library that provide the robust intellectual underpinnings of the new Story of Value.

A NOTE ABOUT THE EDITORS

This Oral Essays collection has been edited by students of the new Story of CosmoErotic Humanism. Each of us has actively participated in *One Mountain, Many Paths*, and most of us have been in deep "Holy of Holies" study with Dr. Marc Gafni for many years.

We have been privileged to find ourselves well-versed in the teachings, and even emerging as lineage-holders of CosmoErotic Humanism.[3]

We view this editing project as a privilege and a deep practice of study and clarification. We experience ourselves as a *mystical editing society*, frequently meeting and conversing together about the content—the depth of knowledge and wisdom offered here—as well as the technical intricacies involved with publishing a beautiful and coherent series of books. In so doing, we function as a "Unique Self Symphony," which itself is a Dharmic

---

3   CosmoErotic Humanism is a world philosophical movement aimed at reconstructing the collapse of value at the core of global culture. Much like Romanticism or Existentialism, CosmoErotic Humanism is not merely a theory but a movement that changes the very mood of Reality. It is an invitation to participate in evolving the source code of consciousness and culture towards a cosmocentric *ethos* for a planetary civilization.

The term CosmoErotic Humanism, initially coined by Dr. Gafni and colleagues, points to a complex, multi-faceted, layered, and nuanced evolutionary set of insights that has evolved over decades of intensive research, teaching, and spiritual practice from deep within a wide range of wisdom traditions (including the Wisdom of Solomon lineage tradition, Bodhisattva Buddhism, and Kashmir Shaivism), as well as multiple disciplines including complexity theory, chaos theory, emergence theory, molecular biology, and the more classical disciplines of the humanities.

The seeds of CosmoErotic Humanism were planted with Dr. Marc Gafni's work on a two-volume, 1,000-page opus called *Radical Kabbalah* (Integral Publishers, 2012). This scholarly work, sourced from deep study within the esoteric lineage texts of the Wisdom of Solomon, points to a non-dual, or acosmic, realization which—unlike the prevailing conceptualization of non-duality—does not efface the human being; rather, it is highly humanistic in its nature. The next step in the evolution of CosmoErotic Humanism was the insight that all of Reality is evolving Eros, which lives in, as, and through the human being.

A failure of Eros leads inexorably to the creation of narratives of "pseudo-eros." CosmoErotic Humanism is a response to the modern mental and social breakdown sourced in the proliferation of multiple forms of pseudo-eros and its broken narratives, such as rivalrous conflict governed by win/lose metrics and the dogmatic denial of intrinsic value in Cosmos, which together generate our current "global intimacy disorder."

term that connotes an omni-considerate collaboration between realized Unique Selves synergizing our unique gifts into a new emergence greater than the sum of the parts. Even as we worked diligently to standardize our editing styles, meeting on a weekly basis to debate the nuances of phrasing, we also operated from within a deep appreciation of the unique style that each editor brought to his or her work. As such, the reader might notice some variation in editing style among the books.

Please note that Dr. Marc Gafni has not reviewed these edited Oral Essays, as he is deeply engaged in writing the formal books of the Great Library. But he has been generous in responding to questions and providing overall guidance in the project. Overall, as Marc's students and students of the *dharma*, we have made it a key project at the Center to publish these pieces of work relatively independently.

OUR UNIQUE ORAL-ESSAY EDITING STYLE PRESERVES THE ENERGY OF THE ORIGINAL TRANSMISSION

Dr. Marc Gafni is a uniquely gifted teacher whose oral transmission is imbued with a quality that has proven transformative for his students. Many of us feel mystically transformed by both the content and the underlying energy of the transmission style. Therefore, as we like to say, *trust the magic ways the dharma comes through your unique understanding!*

As Marc's empowered students, colleagues, and beloved friends, we have a deep knowing that these teachings are vital for the survival and thriving of humanity as we know it, and we recognize the importance of publishing his teachings in a written format that will be accessible by future generations. At the same time, we sought to preserve the Eros of the original oral transmission with all of its nuance, power, and depth. Our intention in the editing process, to the greatest extent possible, has been to keep these spoken artifacts intact in order to maintain the flow of the original transmission. We have therefore chosen not to engage in intensive formal editing, as we found that doing so resulted in the loss of the energetic transmission that is so key to fully receiving the *dharma.*

After experimenting with many ways to present these texts, we developed a specific way of laying out the text on the page. Marc, in collaboration with Zak Stein and Russian intellectual/artist Elena Maslova-Levin—and ultimately all of the editors, through many conversations—developed a unique, artistic presentation of the text, using bolding, italics, bullet points, and other stylistic features which together serve to accentuate the immediacy of the oral transmission.

As part of this editing style, intended to preserve the integrity of the original transmission, we have refrained from removing the frequent recapitulations of key themes. We found that each recapitulation contributes something vital to the rhythm and music beneath the words, like the beating drum of our hearts. These recapitulations not only review previous material but also add important new emphases, perspectives, and elements of the new Story of Value. We ask for your patience as a reader to trust the rhythm of these texts, and we trust you as a reader to have the depth and steadiness to find your way through.

KEY COMPONENTS: LINK TO THE ORIGINAL BROADCAST, EVOLUTIONARY LOVE CODES AND PRAYER

To supplement the written word, each episode includes a QR code linking to the original broadcast on YouTube, as well as occasional links to featured songs and video clips.

Each episode also centers around an "Evolutionary Love Code," formulated by Marc. These codes are part of the ongoing articulation and distillation of the *dharma* as it unfolds and emerges, week by week, over the course of many years, through the mystical process we call Outrageous Love or Evolutionary Love.

Another core component of the *One Mountain, Many Paths* episodes is what Marc and Barbara called "Evolutionary Prayer." Prayer is experienced in *One Mountain* not in the old fundamentalist sense of a "cosmic vending-machine god" who is alienated from Cosmos. Marc refers to this as the "god you do not and should not believe in"—and he often adds, "the god you don't believe in does not exist."

GOD IS THE INFINITE INTIMATE

In fact, in the *dharma* of CosmoErotic Humanism, a new name for God has emerged: the "Infinite Intimate," who appears in first-, second-, and third-person expressions. Marc first shared this name as he heard it whispered in 2023, although earlier intimations and formulations of the name appeared as early as 2010.

In first person, God is infinitely alive and as intimate as our own first-person experience.

In second person, God is the infinitely intimate Personhood of Cosmos that knows our name and holds us—the God about whom we say, *whenever we fall, we fall into Her hands.* This is the God who is our Beloved, Father, Mother, Lover, and Evolutionary Partner.

Finally, in third person, God inheres in all of the First Principles and First Values of Cosmos, and in the laws of science (both interior and exterior) that govern manifest Reality.

Therefore, we have a realization of God as not only the Infinity of Power but also the Infinity of Intimacy.

In *One Mountain, Many Paths*, we are reclaiming prayer at a higher level of consciousness. And we are reclaiming prayer as deep, alive, loving, and intimate conversations with God as the Infinite Intimate who knows our name.

REFLECTING ON THE CO-CREATION BETWEEN DR. MARC GAFNI AND BARBARA MARX HUBBARD

Barbara and Marc met five years before Barbara passed. As Barbara said so often, "before I met Marc, I was sure that I was done." Barbara had taught so beautifully for decades, focusing particularly on a powerful articulation of "conscious evolution." Indeed, it would not be inaccurate to say that Barbara was the greatest storyteller of conscious evolution of her time.

Conscious evolution was also a premise in Marc's thinking, but drawn from an entirely different set of sources and experiences. Barbara drew from the classical sources of evolutionary spirituality, such as Teilhard de Chardin, Buckminster Fuller, and many others. Indeed, she was closely associated with Fuller, and was perhaps de Chardin's most ardent intellectual devotee.

Marc drew a somewhat different vision of conscious evolution from the interior sciences of the great wisdom traditions, with a primary emphasis on what he refers to as the "Solomon lineages," merged together with careful readings of the leading edges of the sciences. In the old version of conscious evolution, the movement from unconscious to conscious was a movement of evolution by chance to evolution by choice. Together Marc and Barbara evolved the old version of Conscious Evolution, pointing out that evolution itself was always in some sense conscious, but as Marc formulated it, the awakening to conscious evolution refers to the awakening of evolution as human consciousness, coupled with the human realization of being conscious evolution in person, and the human capacity to locate oneself within the context of the larger evolutionary story.

Marc focused his attention on an entirely different dimension of Reality, which he and his colleagues began to call CosmoErotic Humanism. The Intimate Universe, Homo amor, Unique Self and Unique Self Symphonies, God as the Infinity of Intimacy, Eros and the CosmoErotic Universe, distinctions like Role Mate, Soul Mate and Whole Mate, the Four Selves, Evolutionary Love, Outrageous Love, Evolution: the Love Story of the Universe, First Principles and First Values, Evolving Perennialism, the Evolution of Love, and many more are terms articulated by Gafni and shared with Barbara in their conversation, study, and creative engagement.

Some terms they coined together, for example "a Planetary Awakening in Love through Unique Self Symphonies," where Gafni described Unique Self Symphonies, and Barbara aligned her vision of a planetary Pentecost to Marc's vision of Unique Self Symphonies.

Other key terms were unique and articulated by Barbara, for example: conscious evolution, teleros, telerotic, from joining genes to joining genius, regenopause, vocational arousal, birthing of humanity, synergy engine, and of course her work around what she called the Wheel of Co-creation. Ultimately, Marc and Barbara attempted to synergize their work in what they called the Wheel of Co-creation 2.0. Barbara and Marc experienced themselves as merging their respective *dharma* into what they began to refer to as Conscious Evolution 2.0, or later, CosmoErotic Humanism.

The first 129 episodes of One Mountain, Many Paths took place in the last period of Barbara's life and reflect the depth and texture of the stunning evolutionary whole-mate meeting between her and Marc. As Barbara was deep in study with Marc, a lot of what she shared in Evolutionary Church was the *dharma* of their deep study and collaboration. Although sometimes it may be clear who is speaking, we generally publish these early episodes in what we are calling "one voice." The first 129 episodes, with Marc and Barbara together, have been grouped chronologically. Episodes 130 to 400 and onwards, which were transmitted by Marc, have been grouped by topic.

THE INVITATION

We invite you to find your way into this revolution. Each one of our Unique Selves and unique gifts are desperately needed as we co-create this new Story of Value together, as part of the covenant between generations, for the sake of the whole.

Let's *play a larger game* and evolve the very source code of consciousness and culture together.

With mad love,

The Editors

LOVE OR DIE

LOCATING OURSELVES: ARTICULATING THE ESSENTIAL CONTEXT FOR THE ONE MOUNTAIN, MANY PATHS ORAL ESSAYS

SETTING OUR INTENTION

Intention setting is everything.

We're here—as da Vinci was with his cohort in the Renaissance—**to play a larger game, to participate in the evolution of love, which is to tell the new Story of Value rooted in First Principles and First Values.**

- ◆ Our intention is to recognize the critical historical juncture in which we find ourselves.
- ◆ Our intention is to take our seat at the table of history and to say, *we take responsibility for this.*
- ◆ Our intention is to participate as revolutionaries for the sake of the whole.

What we're here to do is revolution; revolution for the sake of the evolution of love.

It's a revolution for the sake of the trillions of unborn lives that will not manifest:

- The unborn loves
- The unborn creativity
- The unborn goodness
- The unborn truth
- The unborn beauty

All of it looks to us.

Not because we're engaged in grandiosity. Not at all!

- We're trembling before She.
- We're trembling with joy at the privilege.
- We're trembling with joy at the responsibility.
- We're trembling with joy at the Possibility of Possibility.
- We have to enact a new Story in this moment of time. Because it is only a new Story that can change the vector of history.

The most revolutionary act that we can do—the greatest moral imperative of this time—**is to articulate a new Story at this time between worlds and this time between stories.**

Story is not made up, as postmodernity suggests. **We all live in inescapable frameworks; our framework is the story we live in.** Right now, Reality lives according to win/lose metrics, a story that is generating existential risk. **We need to change that story.**

When we change that story, when we tell a new Story—not a made-up story, but a new Story of Value, rooted in First Principles and First Values—**then it all changes.**

We need to participate in the evolution of the source code of consciousness and culture, which is the evolution of love.

It's the most important, exciting, evolutionary, revolutionary act that we can do to alleviate suffering: to be lovers.

Like Rumi, the great poet of Sufism, we have to be "mad lovers," because it's the only sanity.

To be mad lovers is to see around the corner, to not be so obsessed with the details of the contractions of my life.

Let me see bigger.

Let me take complete care of myself in every possible way, let me completely attend to those in my circle of intimacy and influence, and then—*let me expand my circle.*

That's what we're here for.

- Our intention is to participate in the *LoveForce*, the *LoveIntelligence*, the *LoveBeauty*, the *LoveDesire* that literally animates Cosmos all the way up and all the way down.
- Our intention is to participate in the evolution of love.

  [*In the next few pages we will cover some key concepts which are essential to locating ourselves and setting the context for all the One Mountain, Many Paths Oral Essays. —Ed.*]

OVERVIEW: EROS IS NO LONGER A LUXURY—IT'S LOVE OR DIE

Eros is life.

The failure of Eros destroys life.

Our lack of Eros is poised to destroy the world.

All civilizations have fallen because the stories that they lived in were, in some sense, stories based on rivalrous conflict governed by win/lose metrics. Every civilization was weakened by interior polarization caused by the lack of a shared Story of Value.

We now have a global civilization, but we haven't created a shared Story of Value.

We haven't solved the generator functions that caused all civilizations to fall. Our global civilization has exponential technologies and extraction models depleting the Earth of resources that took billions of years to create, which is going to lead to a civilizational collapse.

Existential risk is risk to our very existence.

The choice is clear: love or die.

It's that simple.

Eros is no longer a luxury. It is an absolute necessity for the survival of the individual and the planet.

In the last half a century, modern psychology has documented an age-old truth: a fully nourished baby who is not held in loving arms will die.

So too, our world, both personal and global—even with all the resources of intelligence and technology at our disposal—will die without being held in love, in the embrace of Eros.

We must embrace a personal path of love and a global politics of love.

Not ordinary love. Not love which is "mere human sentiment," but Eros, or what we sometimes call Outrageous Love, which is the heart of existence itself.

We live in a world of outrageous pain.

The only response is Outrageous Love.

WHAT IS EROS?

Eros is the experience of radical aliveness, moving towards, seeking, desiring ever-deeper contact and ever-greater wholeness.[4] Eros is the core fabric of Reality's being and the motivational architecture of Reality's becoming.

Eros is what animates the evolutionary impulse itself, from the very inception of Cosmos all the way to our very selves, who awaken to the realization that the evolutionary impulse throbs uniquely in each of us.

The realization of human awakening and transformation that lies at the core of the interior sciences is the invitation—or even the urgent and desperate demand—of a madly loving Cosmos animated by infinities of power and infinities of intimacy.

The demand—the desperate invitation, the plea, the tender and fierce command of Cosmos that lives inside every human being—is to awaken: to awaken to our true nature as unique incarnations of Eros and Ethos that are needed and desperately desired by All-That-Is. Said slightly differently: Reality is Eros. Or: God is Eros.

The failure of Eros destroys life. The collapse of Eros is always the hidden (or not so hidden) root cause for the collapse of ethics.

This is true both personally and collectively. We live in a moment of a world-wide and personal collapse of Eros. Our lack of Eros is poised to destroy

---

4 We define Eros through what we refer to as the Eros equation (one of a series of what we call interior science equations):

Eros = Radical Aliveness x Desiring (Growing + Seeking) x Deeper Contact x Greater Wholeness x Self Actualization/Self Transcendence (Creation [Destruction])

There are good reasons for the formal language of the interior science equations in these writings, and the reader is invited to explore them on their own, in particular, in our work, David J. Temple, *First Principles and First Values: Forty-Two Propositions on CosmoErotic Humanism, the Meta-Crisis, and the World to Come* (World Philosophy and Religion, 2024).

the world. Humanity is currently experiencing what has come to be known as existential risk, a risk to our very existence, or what I will refer to as the Second Shock of Existence.

EXISTENTIAL RISK: THE SECOND SHOCK OF EXISTENCE

The first shock of existence is the death of the human being—the realization that we will die, which dawns in human consciousness at the beginning of history. We are not talking about the biological fact of death but the *existential* realization of death. Although the interior sciences disclose that death is a portal between two days (there is vast empirical,[5] philosophical,[6] and anthro-ontological evidence[7] for the continuity of consciousness[8]), death is also, in our own direct surface experience, a stark end. And that is obviously not a bug but a feature in the system.

---

5   We refer to evidence gathered by the most serious of researchers, beginning with Henry and Edith Sedgwick at Cambridge University and William James at Harvard University, and continuing in highly rigorous form for the last 150 years, as recapitulated by Whiteheadian scholar David Ray Griffin in multiple volumes. See also, for example, Dean Radin, *Real Magic: Unlocking Your Natural Psychic Abilities to Create Everyday Miracles* (Potter/TenSpeed/Harmony, 2018), *The Conscious Universe: The Scientific Truth of Psychic Phenomena* (HarperCollins, 2010), and other books. Or see the earlier classic by Frederic William Henry Myers, *Human Personality and Its Survival of Bodily Death* (Longmans, Green, 1907).

6   This requires a cogent analysis of materialism and dualism, and the introduction of the far more cogent third possibility which we have called "pan-interiority."

7   We discuss Anthro-Ontology in some depth in *First Principles and First Values*, and see also the fuller conversation in David J. Temple, *First Principles and First Values: Towards an Evolving Perennialism: Introducing the Anthro-Ontological Method*—both published by World Philosophy and Religion Press, in Conjunction with Integral Publishers. For now, we will simply define it as an "innate and clear interior gnosis directly available to the human being."

8   See Dr. Marc Gafni and Dr. Zachary Stein's essay in preparation, "Beyond Death: Anthro-Ontology, Philosophy, and Empiricism." This essay is slated to appear in the book *Towards a World Religion: Homo Amor Essays*. The essay is also the ground for a larger book by the same authors, *Twelve Portals to Life Beyond Death: Responding to the Second Shock of Existence*, in which we discuss three forms of material: the empirical, the philosophical, and the anthro-ontological, and show how each form discredits the notion of death as the end.

Our first-person experience is that death ends this life. It is not the *totality* of our experience if we go deeper inside, but it is obviously intended to be the central, potent, and painful dimension of every human life. Indeed, as Ernest Becker potently reminded us, the denial of death is at our peril.

All the stories and all the plotlines and all the threads of living end at that moment. Whatever happens beyond, we have an actual experience of ending. **Paradoxically, that ending, the experience of the finality of mortality, is what presses us into life.** From the implicit demand of the first shock of existence, human beings were activated and pressed into creative emergence, and what emerged was all of human culture, both interior and exterior.

The second shock of existence is the realization of the potential death of all humanity. After all the stages of human history—matter, life, and mind in all of their stages of evolutionary unfolding—we have come to this place in the evolution of humanity, in which the gap between our exponentially expanding exterior technologies and our stalled (or even regressing) interior technologies of value has created dire catastrophic and existential risks.

This gap generates extraction models and exponential growth curves, rivalrous conflicts based on win/lose metrics, tragedies of the commons, and multipolar traps, in which everyone has to keep producing to the nth degree, including weaponized exponential threats to our very existence because we are afraid that the other parties are going to do it and not be transparent—hide it from us and then dominate us.

GENERATOR FUNCTIONS FOR EXISTENTIAL RISK

Let's outline clearly the main *generator functions for existential risk.*

Rivalrous conflicts governed by zero-sum, win/lose metrics. Rivalrous conflicts generate extraction models at the core of the economic system and exponential growth curves. Both of these drive and are driven by a contrived system of artificially manufactured desires and needs, delivered into culture by ever more precise forms of micro-targeting to individuals and groups through the ever more immersive environment of the internet.

Next, rivalrous conflicts and exponential growth curves animated by win/lose metrics generate **complicated, fragile world systems** highly vulnerable to myriad forms of collapse. Fragile local systems are made exponentially more fragile on a global level by our inability to meet global challenges with social, legal, political, economic, and ethical infrastructures that remain largely local.

All of this is a direct result of the failure to develop more adequate interior technologies that would be sufficiently compelling to displace "rivalrous conflict governed by win/lose metrics" as the motivational architecture for the human life world.

This failure has led to the conditions that will cause the implosion of systems that are already and quite literally on the brink of collapsing themselves. That's what we mean by the *second shock of existence.*

To recapitulate: the second shock of existence is not the death of the human being, but the potential death of humanity.

It is the *Death Star* moment of our species.

THE DECONSTRUCTION OF INTRINSIC VALUE

We stand in this moment poised between utopia and dystopia, at a time between worlds and a time between stories. We need a new Story of Value, eternal yet evolving, rooted in First Principles and First Values, which would become a universal grammar of value and a context for our diversity.

This is exactly what the Renaissance was. It was a time between worlds and a time between stories. In the Renaissance, we had recently been challenged by the Black Death, a pandemic that swept across Europe. The Black Death destroyed between a third to half of Europe and a huge part of

Asia. People died horrifically, brutally, in the streets. They had no idea how to meet this challenge, and so, in response to the Black Death, da Vinci and Ficino and their cohorts understood that they had to tell a new Story of Value.

That story was the story of modernity. Did they get it right?

- They got part of it right, which birthed, to use Jürgen Habermas' phrase, "the dignities of modernity," such as new ways of gathering information and universal human rights.
- But they also deconstructed the source of Value. They lost the basis for the Good, the True, and the Beautiful.

The basis used to be divine revelation: *God told us.* But this claim was owned by religion, and every religion began to overreach and over-claim. The revelation was thus often mediated through cultural categories and wasn't fully accurate.

Modernity threw out revelation, but was unable to establish a new basis for value.

Value was just assumed to be real. As it says in the founding document of the American Revolution: *We hold these truths to be self-evident*—that is, *we don't really have a basis for value; we just take it as a given.*

In other words, modernity took out a loan of social capital from the traditional world. The source of value was never worked out.

And then, gradually, value began to collapse.

- The Universe Story began to collapse.
- The belief that the Good, the True, and the Beautiful are real began to collapse.
- The belief that Love is real began to collapse.

As Bertrand Russell is reported to have said, "I cannot see how to refute the arguments for the subjectivity of ethical values, but I find myself incapable of believing that all that is wrong with wanton cruelty is that I do not like it."

What do you do if you grew up in a world in which value is not real? A world without a source of value, without a Universe Story, without a story of human identity, without a story of desire, without a narrative of power?

In the words of W.B. Yeats, *the center does not hold.*

- You have a collapse at the very center of society, because you no longer have Eros.
- You no longer have a Reality in which value is real, and so you have this lingering sense of emptiness.
- You have a complete collapse at the very center.
- We become *the hollow men and the stuffed men*, gesture without form.

And that's the source of our current existential risk.

THE DEEPER ROOT CAUSE OF THE META-CRISIS: A GLOBAL INTIMACY DISORDER

Above, I have outlined the major generator functions of existential risk. But there is a deeper cause for the existential risk that lurks underneath the rivalrous conflict governed by win/lose metrics and the fragile systems they engender.

And we cannot take the Death Star down without discerning and addressing this. We have already alluded to this root cause above, but at this point we need to make it more explicit so that, from this context, the adequate root response will become clear.

Modernity threw out the revelation, but was unable to establish a new basis for value.

This ostensibly surprising statement can be understood in a few simple steps:

1. All of the catastrophic and existential risk challenges we face are global: from climate change to artificial intelligence, pandemics, systems collapse, and exponential arms races.
2. Every global challenge self-evidently requires a global solution.
3. Global solutions can only be implemented with global co-ordination.
4. Global co-ordination is impossible without global coherence.
5. Global coherence is only possible if there is a global resonance between the parts.
6. Global resonance is only possible if we have global intimacy.

ONLY A SHARED STORY OF VALUE CAN GENERATE GLOBAL INTIMACY

Global intimacy—just like intimacy in a couple—is only possible when there is a shared story.

Not just a shared history, but a shared Story of Value.

- It is only a shared global story that can generate a new emergent quality of intimacy: global intimacy.
- A shared Story of Value must be rooted in shared ordinating values, or what we have called evolving First Values and First Principles.
- Intimacy requires a shared grammar of value as a matrix for a shared Story of Value.

The global intimacy disorder is the root cause for existential risk. The global intimacy disorder underlies the core generator functions for existential risk.

The global intimacy disorder is rooted in the failure to experience ourselves in a field of shared intrinsic value. This failure derives from the deconstruction of value.

Indeed, it is wholly accurate to say that **the root cause of the two generator functions of existential risk is the failed story of intrinsic value, or what we might also call the breakdown of Eros.**

1. The first generator function is **the success story**. Our modern success story is rivalrous conflict governed by win/lose metrics, which violates all the terms of the Intimacy Equation: there is no shared identity and no mutuality of recognition, feeling, value or purpose, and instead of *relative* otherness, there is *alienated* otherness. Such a story generates complicated fragile systems with no allurement or intimacy between the parts, systems which optimize for efficiency (as an expression of win/lose metrics) and not for resiliency and life.

2. The second generator function is **the deconstruction of intrinsic value** itself. The deconstruction of value is the sense that human value does not participate in the intrinsic value of the Real, for the Real is dogmatically declared to have no intrinsic value. Thus, there is no shared identity between the interior of the human being and Reality. There is no common participation in a field of shared intrinsic value. Instead of being intimate with value, we are alienated from value. And only intrinsic value can arouse will: political, moral, and social will.

To sum up, without a shared grammar of value there is no global intimacy, and therefore no global coherence, and no global coordination in response to catastrophic and existential risk, which means, put simply, there will be, quite literally, no future.

HEALING THE GLOBAL INTIMACY DISORDER REQUIRES THE EVOLUTION OF INTIMACY

But we are not hopeless. On the contrary, we are filled with great hope. Hope is a memory of the future. That memory of the future *is* the direct hit that takes down the Death Star, the culture of death. **The direct hit must be**—as it has always been in history—**the emergence of a new stage of evolution**.

Crisis is an evolutionary driver, and every crisis is, at its core, a crisis of intimacy: from the oxygen crisis of the single cells dying which generated multicellular life at the dawn of existence, to the existential risk in this very moment.[9]

The direct hit is therefore structurally self-evident: the evolution of intimacy itself.

What is intimacy, as a structure of Cosmos all the way down and all the way up the evolutionary chain? We engage this inquiry in depth in other writings, but for now we will simply adduce what we have called the "Intimacy Equation":

Intimacy = shared identity in the context of [relative] otherness x mutuality of recognition x mutuality of pathos x mutuality of value x mutuality of purpose

Intimacy is about the capacity of parts to generate a *shared identity* while retaining their otherness, or distinct identity. This requires multiple mutualities, including recognition, pathos (or feeling), value, and purpose. The parts must recognize and feel each other, even as they share value and purpose. But all of this must lead to intimate union—and not pathological

---

9 We demonstrate this principle in some depth in the multi-volume series, *The Universe: A Love Story* (forthcoming) (https://worldphilosophyandreligion.org/early-ontologies), *The Intimate Universe: Global Intimacy Disorder as Cause for Global Action Paralysis* (forthcoming), and in other writings of CosmoErotic Humanism.

fusion, where the distinct identity of the parts disappears—like subatomic particles that successfully become an atom, or two people who successfully become a couple.

THE DECONSTRUCTION OF VALUE IS THE DECONSTRUCTION OF INTIMACY

We have identified the global intimacy disorder as the root cause of existential risk. But the underlying ultimate failure of intimacy is the deconstruction of value itself.

The deconstruction of value means that human value does not participate in any sense of intrinsic value of the Real. This is not about individual *values*, but about *the Field of Value* that underlies all of them. **When the human being**—moved, often sincerely or even nobly, by myriad cultural, historical, and psychological confusions—**claims to have stepped out of the Field of Value, then intimacy itself is deconstructed.**

The deconstruction of value is the deconstruction of intimacy.

In the absence of a shared Story of Value, a story that is an authentic expression of Reality's Eros, a story rooted in *pseudo-Eros* takes center stage and becomes the generator function for existential risk. Our modern pseudo-Eros story is *rivalrous conflict governed by win/lose metrics*. Such a story catalyzes in its wake the second generator function of existential risk: *complicated fragile systems with no allurement or intimacy between the parts*. It is in that sense that we have argued that the first generator function for existential risk is the success story.

- The failure of intimacy is precisely the impotent experience that there is no shared identity between the interior of the human being and Reality. **There is no shared identity in the sense of any kind of common participation in a field of shared intrinsic value.**
- **But only a shared Story of Value can arouse the global will**

required to engage catastrophic and existential risk. For it is only global political, moral, and social will—and we can even say *erotic* will—that can generate the most Good, True and Beautiful world that we have always known is possible.

THE EVOLUTION OF LOVE IS THE TELLING OF A NEW STORY

Coupled with the Intimacy Equation is the scientifically grounded realization, in both the exterior and interior sciences, that Reality is a progressive deepening of intimacies, or, said slightly differently:

Reality is Evolution. Evolution is the evolution of intimacy.

- The evolution of intimacy requires—both personally and collectively—a deeper, more accurate discernment of the nature of our universe, ourselves, and our beloveds.
- This new discernment generates a new global Story of Value.
- The new global Story of Value generates an emergent, heretofore unseen global intimacy and heals the global intimacy disorder.

The new Story of Value is the direct hit that takes down the Death Star and replaces it with the hope that invokes the memory of our best future.

Global intimacy facilitates global coherence, which facilitates global coordination, which activates the possibility of our creative and effectively coordinated global responses to the global meta-crisis in its entirety and its specific expressions.

To solve Bertrand Russell's challenge—the apparent argument for the subjectivity of ethical values—**we have to reground value theory in eternal yet evolving First Principles and First Values, and articulate a new Story of Value.**

This is what we call CosmoErotic Humanism.

CosmoErotic Humanism—together with other emergent strands—**needs to become the ground of a world religion as a context for our diversity**. We need religion, even as we need science, to articulate a shared global grammar of value.

As we said at the beginning, our choice is simple: love or die.

- To love means to participate in the evolution of love, which is the evolution of the human Story of Value.
- To love means to evolve and activate a new cultural enlightenment—rooted in a new narrative of identity, a new narrative of value, a new narrative of intimate communion, a new narrative of desire, a new narrative of power—all of which will birth new narratives of economics and politics.
- The evolution of love is the telling of a new Story.

The new Story that must be told is a love story, for in fact that is the deepest truth of Reality, rooted in the best exterior and interior sciences, that we have at this moment in time:

- Reality is not merely a fact. Reality is a story.
- Reality is not an ordinary story. Reality is a love story.
- Reality is not an ordinary love story. Reality is an Outrageous Love Story.

Story doesn't mean it's *made-up*.

It means doing the hard work of integrating the validated insights of the traditional world, the modern world, and the postmodern world.

This is the intention at the heart of telling the new Story of CosmoErotic Humanism.

EDITOR'S PREFACE

The content of this book is based on live talks given by Dr. Marc Gafni and Barbara Marx Hubbard on the weekly sensemaking podcast of Evolutionary Church, now known as One Mountain, Many Paths. The style adopts a spoken-word approach rather than a formal essay, combining the voices of both teachers into a cohesive narrative. By unifying the voices and maintaining the energy of spoken word, we highlight the joy, delight, rigor, and depth of Dr. Marc Gafni and Barbara Marx Hubbard as a united, evolutionary, whole mate pair who connect us to the intrinsic values of Reality.

In its entirety, Dr. Marc Gafni and Barbara Marx Hubbard invite us to embrace what they have called a new Story of Value rooted in First Principles and First Values. In the Evolutionary Church that they founded, they sought explicitly to enact a new world philosophy and religion rooted in the tenets of Evolutionary Love, ecstatically urging us to consciously align with the evolutionary impulse.

A planetary awakening in love envisions the birth of a new species, *Homo amor*, and the emergence of societies capable of loving, transcending the illusion of a separate self, and aligning with the whole, all while recognizing each individual as a unique expression of the divine process of creation. And of course, the Evolutionary Church was articulated by Marc and Barbara as the most potent possible response to the meta-crisis of existential risk that we are now facing. Every week, they taught that, as Marc said, "No detail of our lives is disconnected from cosmic magnificence… And in that realization, we begin to realize our true nature, and we become omni-considerate, omni-loving, and omni-responsible for the whole."

I vividly recall the day I became aware that my personal growth process carries cosmic significance.

Decades before, my originally unaware journey towards enlightenment began as efforts to liberate myself from severe self-hatred and destructive addiction through twelve-step programs. After a few years, I transitioned to a lifestyle of peer counseling, committing myself to healing my mind and body from the tremendous suffering I lived with. Through hard work and devoted healing, in 1998, I established a thriving global company that still empowers countless people to improve the quality of their lives.

Still, a deep yearning persisted within me. I encountered Christian mystics who introduced me to the transformative power of living my journey at the intersection between trauma and spirituality. Subsequently, I formed an intimate connection with a beloved Native American friend, who encouraged me to dive deeply into the Mystery. Still, my longing for something more remained unfulfilled. One night, while watching an episode of *Cosmos* with Neil deGrasse Tyson, exploring the domestication of wolves, coyotes, and foxes into dogs, a realization sparked in me that was well beyond the content of the show—my personal growth could also be an evolutionary process.

Following this revelation, I conducted an online search for the correlation between personal growth and evolution, which led me to discover the ideas of Conscious Evolution by Barbara Marx Hubbard. I knew it! I felt it in my very core: I am an integral part of the ongoing evolution of the entire cosmos. But there was something still missing from the teaching. Then Barbara joined forces with the visionary Dr. Marc Gafni. Marc's teaching brought Conscious Evolution to the next level, what he called CosmoErotic Humanism. Barbara and Marc initiated The Planetary Awakening Accelerator, for the sake of evolving the source code of consciousness and culture. I eagerly joined the year-long intensive, recognizing the opportunity to further deepen my understanding of what it means to be a human being and how to actively contribute to creating the most beautiful, true, and good future possible.

At some point, it all deepened immeasurably. I had asked Reality for a teacher, and I knew that Marc, who incarnates the alive, tender, and fierce heart of CosmoErotic Humanism and shows up with radical rigor, depth, demand, and devotion, was to be my teacher. Marc's sense of teaching is profoundly anti-guru and as such he always demands my power and autonomy and consistently invites me to find my own voice and depth.

Weekly, for years now, we have studied sacred text together, diving deep into the wisdom traditions and the evolution of love. Since embracing this *dharma*—some of the seeds of which are within this text—I continue my journey as a student and lineage holder, fulfilling my unique role with Barbara and Marc as an evolutionary co-creator.

Over the last years, Evolutionary Church has deepened and evolved and become a thriving community that we now call One Mountain, Many Paths. We are committed together to participating in the creation of the Great Library of CosmoErotic Humanism at the Center for World Philosophy and Religion. The mission of the center, co-led by Dr. Marc and Dr. Zachary Stein, together with me and many other partners, is what Marc and Barbara call a Planetary Awakening in Love through Unique Self Symphonies.

In this text, we are going to be audacious, and we are going to reach as far as we can. We serve the more conscious and loving world, and I am beyond honored to have been able to edit these spoken-word transcripts and bring them to the holy reader.

I invite you to embark on this journey with us. Let us raise a toast to Love. May these teachings, or *dharma*, fill you in all their evolutionary ways, as they continually do for me.

In devotion,

Kristina Tahel Amelong

ABOUT THIS VOLUME

We live in a world of outrageous pain, and the only response to outrageous pain is Outrageous Love. Somehow, we know inside that this is true. The deepest pleasure of being alive is to recognize that Reality is an Outrageous Love Story.

This book is about a Planetary Awakening in Love, the emergence from *Homo sapiens* to *Homo amor*. As humans we are here to articulate and enact a new story, to participate in the evolution of love itself. With practice we can learn to place our attention on the evolutionary impulse that is alive and awake in us, as us, and through us, and calling us forth to become Evolutionary Lovers.

In this book, we are reclaiming practices of prayer, intimacy, and the sacred as part of a new politics of Evolutionary Love. This is the only way for us to move beyond separation towards a planetary coherence of synergy and wholeness.

This book explores the essential question: Who are you? The response is both simple and complex: You are an irreducibly unique expression of the Evolutionary LoveIntelligence of Reality itself, and as such you have a unique gift to give to the world, that only you can give! Each of us is an irreducibly unique expression of the LoveIntelligence and LoveBeauty of All-That-Is, with a unique gift to give in the Unique Self Symphony.

Through the lens of Evolutionary Spirituality, it becomes clear that the Universe is not a random accident. Not at all. It is an Evolutionary Love Story, moving towards ever greater intimacy and ever greater wholeness. We are personally implicated in the great story of Reality, holding the power to transform crisis into possibility through the force of Outrageous

Love. As we move into the fullness of our humanity, our personal story emerges as a chapter and verse in the Love Story of Reality itself.

Loneliness is a profound evolutionary driver, urging us to move beyond isolation into deeper connection and to say YES to the impulse of evolution within us. We are not meant to walk this path alone. The move from loneliness to loving takes us beyond the illusion of separation, and we find ourselves woven into the fabric of Unique Self Symphony.

Practice helps us to connect with the sacred at a higher level of consciousness, reclaiming devotion, evolutionary prayer, and the radical knowing that we are held by God as the Infinity of Intimacy.

Together we join genius in Unique Self Symphony—where each unique voice is radically needed, and each unique gift is desired by All-That-Is. We stand at the edge of history, as Evolutionary Lovers and co-creators of a new humanity. We learn to say *Yes* to the impulse of Evolutionary Love within us, to recognize that we are not separate but part of an interconnected field of intimacy, responsibility, and transformation.

Are you ready to step into this next great moment of human becoming? To say *Yes* to the evolutionary impulse within you? To respond to the crisis of our time with the only force great enough to meet it—Outrageous Love?

If your heart has brought you to explore this path, welcome to the Planetary Awakening in Love through Unique Self Symphonies!

Volume 1

These oral essays are edited talks delivered by
Marc Gafni and Barbara Marx Hubbard between
October and December 2016.

CHAPTER ONE

NURTURING THE UNION OF HUMANS AND THE EVOLUTIONARY IMPULSE

Episode 1 — October 29, 2016

THE EMERGENCE OF THE NEW HUMAN AND THE NEW HUMANITY

We are becoming sensitive to the evolutionary impulse that—for billions and billions of years—has been creating the Universe, Earth, life, animal life, human life, and now *evolutionary human life.*

We need to nurture this deeper union of humans and the Divine as we continue to gain the powers we used to attribute to the gods. We have gained the power:

- To grow worlds
- To destroy worlds
- To create bodies
- To destroy bodies

Where do we get the inner guidance to live at this threshold of evolution, to access within ourselves the deeper patterns of creation that are running through every one of us, as our Unique Self? How do we actually incarnate

1

the process of evolution, now that we've been given the power of very young godlings?

It has been said that we are created in the image of God, and it seems that we are becoming ever more godlike. And yet, to become good gods, loving gods, gods expressing the process of creation, we need to evoke together a Field of Resonance, a resourcing with Source, so that our hearts are opening and vibrating with the frequency of the impulse of creation.

At the threshold of evolution, or what we call Conscious Evolution, we are creating a Field of Resonance for those who are called to be co-evolvers and co-creators of a world equal to our creative, personal, social, scientific, and technological potential.

- It is the emergence of a new human.
- It is the emergence of an evolutionary humanity.
- It is the birth of ourselves in a planetary awakening through a Unique Self Symphony in which everybody's note, everybody's voice, everybody's frequency, is resonating together in this field.

There's a joy, hope, wonder, love, and goodness that is in each one of us to give as we nurture our union with the Divine.

RECLAIMING PRAYER AT HIGHER LEVELS OF CONSCIOUSNESS

Prayer is a word that we're not used to using in the world of evolutionary spirituality. We have let prayer be hijacked: *Prayer is for those fundamentalists. Prayer is for those who aren't sophisticated. Prayer is for those who don't realize that we are really God ourselves.*

We want to participate together in evolving the source code of culture and consciousness, reclaiming what we mean by prayer at higher levels of consciousness.

On the one hand, prayer is attunement.

- We understand that Reality, Source, the evolutionary impulse turns to us and says, *Be my partner.*
- We understand that the great flaring forth of the Big Bang, incarnating the divine impulse, turns to us and says, *I can't do it without you.*
- We understand that creativity is not just *without* but *within.* That there is an incessant, ceaseless creativity, which is the very Eros of Cosmos coming alive in us—uniquely.

We attune to that field, that Field of Resonance, that Field of Evolutionary Imperative, that Field of the Evolutionary Impulse which lives and awakens in us, as us, and through us.

But not prayer to a God who is merely *without* on whom we must rely because we have no powers. No! We're at the end of the era where God is *only without*, where we are but to be obedient, where we are but to fulfill the decree.

God in the first person:

- God, living in me, as me, and through me.
- God, as the evolutionary impulse, awakening uniquely in me.

We drop to our knees.

We let go of our arrogance.

We let go of the sense that we are not gods.

We fall on our knees before the LoveIntelligence and LoveBeauty of Cosmos that existed before we ever began to think.

We bow before the LoveIntelligence of Cosmos that manifested photosynthesis in the great symphony of mitosis and meiosis, before there was ever a neocortex, let alone human brains, which all the super computers and all the scientists in the world can't dream of.

3

We bow in delight and in devotion because we want to reclaim devotion and prayer. We claim our powers. We claim our powers as divine miniatures. And we bow.

This reclaiming of devotion—together with the claiming of our powers and responsibility—is the essence of the planetary awakening.

So, what does it mean to pray?

Does Reality, does God, hear prayer?

The pointing out instructions are as follows:

> *When you speak, do we hear your voice?*
>
> *We do. You speak and others hear.*

But, *how do we hear*? Merely through the physical structures within the ear? Of course, those physical structures are necessary, but what hears you, understands you, is able to receive you, is moved by you?

What hears you, what is moved by you, is divine intelligence, divine essence.

Is there a larger intelligence, that's larger than our personal intelligence, hearing? Of course there is.

Our essence, our intelligence that hears, participates in the larger intelligence of Cosmos.

Just like when we do push-ups our power is connected to the Field of Infinite Power, which is alive in us. Our power participates in the larger power of Cosmos, which is a weightlifter who's stronger than us, stronger than jet propulsion, stronger than all the forces of Cosmos exponentialized.

The larger power is infinite power, in which we participate.

When we hear each other with our intelligence, our intelligence participates in the LoveIntelligence of Cosmos. If our personal intelligence can hear, and if our intelligence participates—is not separate from—the larger Field of LoveIntelligence, then **we are being heard by the Field of LoveIntelligence itself.**

For that which hears in us is not merely our ears but this larger Field of LoveIntelligence. Our intelligence cannot be split from the larger Field of LoveIntelligence. Thus, if our intelligence hears, then the larger Field of LoveIntelligence hearts.

It is that simple. Is it at all possible that the Universe can't hear? Does the Universe suddenly go unintelligent? We don't think so. This is true, self-evidently true that:

When we speak, Reality hears. God is Reality and Reality is God. The god you don't believe in doesn't exist.

Let go of those small visions of God.

When your mother was pounding on the door, and you were six years old, she said, *I'm going to punish you, God's going to open the door; unlock it right now!*

That god doesn't exist.

God is:

- ◆ The Infinity of Intimacy
- ◆ The infinite power of Cosmos that knows our name
- ◆ The evolutionary impulse that beats in our chest
- ◆ The LoveIntelligence that knows our name and holds us in every moment

The new name of God that we have articulated in the great new Story of Value—what we call CosmoErotic Humanism is—The Infinite Intimate.

The name of God is the *Infinite Intimate.*

Kant wrote that moderns are embarrassed by prayer. But this is prayer to the old cosmic vending-machine God. What we are doing is evolving prayer as part of the evolution of consciousness which is the evolution of love.

We reclaim prayer at a higher level of consciousness. We humbly invite everyone, with our hearts open, to open your heart. We put our hands on our hearts. It's a practice of CosmoErotic Humanism. We put our hands on our heart physically, as if we are opening a door, either the left hand or the right hand. We actually open our hearts. Ah! We open our hearts.

Our heart participates in the divine heart. God is the heart of Cosmos.

We invite everyone to pray. Maybe we haven't prayed for many, many years. Many of us erroneously think God, or the infinite LoveIntelligence of Reality that manifested mitosis and meiosis before there was ever a scientist or a supercomputer, we think that intelligence of Reality is too busy to be concerned with *our* life.

Well, that is not true.

A great master said, *Ask for everything; ask for everything.*

We matter individually.

Self-love means to know that all of Reality intended our existence and that *we* matter—infinitely.

We invite everyone to pray. Anything you want to pray for—for yourself, for anyone, for the world, for the environment.

We stop. We pray. We pray together.

Feel prayer rising as evolution.

Wow, please help me be a better partner.

Please help me ask for forgiveness.

Please help me make enough money to support my family.

Please help me find my creativity.

Thank God, wrote Michael Dowd, in his book, *Thank God for Evolution*. The great story of the Divine unfolding in us, as us, and through us.

THE EXILE OF LOVE

We have exiled love as well, haven't we?

Love has been exiled to the merely romantic, or to the merely sexual, and we've forgotten that that's not what love is.

Love is so much deeper.

Love lives everywhere.

We want to be in love now—together.

We can be loved by each other.

When we reclaim prayer, we want to reclaim it from that place, that place of being beloved to each other.

The inner impulse in us is activating us to experience this prayer, to experience this evolution. This inner impulse is a *frequency*. This inner impulse comes from the source of creation that has been evolving for billions and billions of years—in each one of us.

We are each uniquely coded with the frequency of the entire evolutionary journey that is wanting to come forward now as our own expressions of love, of creativity, of vocation.

Each of us is literally coded with the evolutionary impulse of creation.

Some of the intentions of CosmoErotic Humanism are to create:

- A field for the evolution of humanity
- A space in consciousness
- A space in being with one another where this profound evolutionary impulse in each one of us can come to consciousness

- A space where God gives us guidance, through that impulse, as to our *own unique gift to the world*, as to *our own unique voice*, that we can emerge with others in what we call Unique Self Symphony

Just imagine for a moment, every voice on this planet impelled by the impulse of creation, uniquely in each person:

- Sounding the note of inspiration, of creativity, of desire to give our gift to the whole
- Sounding as a Unique Self Symphony

How does the Unique Self Symphony express itself?

The vision is a Planetary Awakening in Love, the birth of humanity capable of co-evolving with nature, and co-creating with Spirit, to be a birthing place for the co-evolution of humanity.

Our vision awakens in humanity the capability of expressing our spiritual, social, scientific, technological genius. We restore Earth to free the people, to explore the vast regions of cosmic inner space, and to explore the cosmos beyond this planet.

How is this going to happen?

One of the key practices is *prayer*.

Another practice is holding yourself in conscious awareness through meditation.

EVOLUTIONARY CHAKRA MEDITATION

Put your mind in the mind of God at the origin of creation. Imagine that eternal process becoming coded through that Big Bang, and going through the billions of years of evolution. Genius creating life, human life—and now your own life—as an impulse of those billions of years. We're sitting right at the edge of the billions of years.

Bring it right in your base chakra and feel the security of the entire impulse of creation, indwelling as you, as your security, the invisible force within us. Bring those billions of years from the mind of God right up through your base chakra into your generative organs.

Feel yourself shifting from devolution towards evolution, from degeneration toward regeneration.

Feel yourselves being activated, *Oh, there's more for us to do, there's more for us to be.* We are now expressing this process of creation, uphold that impulse once again, breathe it out all the way through the base chakra to the generative organs, and take it into the power center.

The power of the process of creation is in every one of us, uniquely expressing as our own impulse to give, to be, to reach out. Feel the enormity of that power in you. You recognize it's coming from the source of creation, uniquely, as you.

Take one more deep breath in, up through all the chakras through the base chakra to the generative organs. You are regenerating, you are expressing your full power.

Bring it right up into the place where the emotions dwell, the pain, the sorrow, the separation, the feeling of inadequacy. That place where you say, *I'm not good enough, I'll never make it. It won't be me. Where am I going? I don't know what to do.*

Let that impulse, which has direction, which has purpose, which has the knowledge of creation within it, let it go through those emotions. Let it organize and calibrate those emotions into a field in which they go directly into the heart.

All of our emotions, whatever feelings of separation we may have had, let it go into the heart. And in that heart of unconditional love, we find the basic impulse of evolution. Set the intention to bring forth the impulse of Eros in evolution into the heart of all of humanity. Just feel that in your heart, feel the almost infinite expression of love.

Let it out the whole way. We do not need to hold our love of one another back. Let that evolution in your heart go right up into your upper heart, which is your vocation. Your gift of love to the world, your unique expression, your vocation of destiny, what the impulse of evolution is born in you to do.

Let it be not just a personal, separate intention or project. Let it be within a unique expression of the genius of evolution as our own calling, our own vocation. **Let us incarnate the genius of evolution in our expressions in the world. Feel the glory of the empowerment of all of humanity wherever we congregate in the community.** Let us feel it in the communion of the evolutionary potential, that intention of creation in each of us.

Take in one more deep breath. A deep breath from the source of creation all the way up through the genius of evolution, through the lower chakras, through the heart, through the vocation of destiny.

Now, bring it into your voice. Let your voice be the frequency of the impulse of evolution within you. That voice is different from the purely mental mind. It is the voice that holds the quality, the resonance, the frequency of that impulse as you. When you speak it through the planetary symphony, the Unique Self Symphony, when you speak it into the noosphere or the thinking layer of Earth or social media or the internet, you are expressing the voice of creation, as you, into the field.

Then let it go all the way up into your third eye, to the spiritual awakening of almost infinite intelligence pulsing through each one of us. Let us bring it up, bring it down, bring it in, and bring it out.

Nurture the incarnation of the evolutionary impulse as conscious evolutionaries. As beings born at the precise moment when evolution becomes conscious of itself in others, when evolution becomes aware of itself as evolution by choice, by prayer, by intention, by inspiration, by creation, by joining together in love. Our intention is to offer sacred space for people to gather together, to evolve in love, and to give their unique gift to our Unique Self Symphony for a planetary awakening.

The thought of the birth of a co-creative humanity as a planetary awakening in love. It is like the birth of a newborn child, when its nervous system just barely links up. It opens its eyes and, if it's very fortunate, it is held in the arms of its mother. The baby is placed in the mother's arms against the mother's heart. He feels the heartbeat from that mother awakening its nervous system to the realization that it is loved.

Our intention is to generate the awareness that we are loved; that we are created by a universal process of creation that has direction, has purpose, has intention. Its intention is higher consciousness, greater freedom, and more complex and more loving order.

Every impulse in every one of us toward consciousness, freedom, and love, in the Unique Self Symphony, toward a planetary awakening to literally help the world shift from a phase of devolution and crisis to a phase of evolution and co-creation.

- *Everyone* is precious.
- *Every voice* is needed.
- *Every one of us* is orchestrated by the invisible process of creation coming to a new climax in the evolutionary planetary awakening in love, in our lifetime.

AWAKEN TO THE DEEPEST PLEASURE OF BEING ALIVE

We are using words here that are not simple, though, and we are talking about God.

How can we say *God*? How many people have died in the name of God? I can't believe it all.

Yet we use the word *God*. We are reclaiming the word *God*. We're reclaiming the word *prayer*. We are reclaiming the word *church*.

Many people say, *Yes, I love church*. Other people are saying, *No, only use phrases like a spiritual center*.

We are reclaiming a field of language and reinvesting that field with evolutionary intention. We are not politically correct; we are *spiritually* incorrect.

We are not merely to comfort the afflicted, we are to afflict the comfortable because we recognize the distinction between comfort and pleasure. We think the opposite of pain is pleasure, but actually the opposite of pain is *comfort*, to be comfortably numb—remember the song "Comfortably Numb," by Pink Floyd.

We don't want to just be comfortable.

The goal of life in the Western world is so often to live as comfortably as you can, and then you die comfortably numb. But we want to awaken to pleasure. **We want to awaken to the pleasure that drives Cosmos.**

Evolution evolves because it feels good. There's a quantum hedonism at the depth of Reality.

Pleasure doesn't mean ice cream.

Pleasure doesn't mean inappropriate sexuality.

Pleasure doesn't mean the wrong food.

Pleasure means the deepest pleasure of being alive, of living on purpose, of living our *telos* and living our Eros, of living in a Telerotic Universe.

We set our intention for what might be:

- A place that's not merely politically correct but which is spiritually incorrect.
- A place in which the god that you don't believe in doesn't exist.
- A place in which human dignity, men and women, count.
- A place that stands against the idea that the feminine is the

good and the masculine is the bad. Masculine and feminine are both gorgeous. They both have light; they both have shadow and they both live within us.

◆ A place that speaks truth to power and stands in integrity, finds our own mind, and seeks deeper discernment.

HOPE IS A MEMORY OF THE FUTURE

We are about articulating a memory of the future because hope is a memory of the future.

We work to convene—with many other people around the world, all of us together, dozens of people—a citizen's Office for the Future owned by no one, owned by everyone; we want to articulate the memory of the future.

One great master said in his original Aramaic and translated as, *when you wake up in the morning you have to articulate a memory of the future.*

What's our memory of the future?

We are going to do this together.

We're going to rise up together.

We're going to transform together.

The next Buddha is a *sangha* filled with Buddhas. **The next great emergence is not merely mastermind but meta-mind, in which every individual is irreducibly unique and honored. And yet we come together in a collective field of resonance and intelligence, which is not pre-personal but trans-personal.**

Something emerges that is so much greater, synergistically, than the sum of the parts. God dances in our voices as we bow in humility.

Our intention is to create a new language together, or a new *dharma.*

13

WE LIVE IN A WORLD OF OUTRAGEOUS PAIN

We live in a world of outrageous pain, and that is a statement of *dharma*.

By *dharma* we mean the best understanding of Reality we have when we look at Reality with an unflinching eye.

We live in a world of outrageous pain:

- ◆ 17,000 children die of starvation every day in a world that has enough to feed every child four times over.
- ◆ Churches, whether they are New Age platforms or old churches of the old form, are lost in power grabs. Churches are lost in consolidating and commodifying Spirit and selling it back to us.
- ◆ News organizations are worried about being in the black, and they are turning elections into reality television. They are avoiding the deeper places that unite us.

Wow, what's happening?

- ◆ How could it be that we live in a world in which there are two billion people who don't have basic human dignity?
- ◆ How could it be that we live in a world in which hundreds of millions of people go to sleep alone at night, lost in the depth, the depravity of loneliness? In which their unique beauty, that was intended by all of Reality for 13.7 billion years, isn't recognized, delighted in, and honored?
- ◆ How could we live in a world in which we don't recognize that every human being is worthy, and every human being has a story to tell, and to live, to sing, and to celebrate?

Every story needs to be honored.

Every story is dignified.

Every story needs to be received.

Every story is impressed on Reality by the lips of the Divine.

How could we live in a world that's not like that?

We live in a world of outrageous pain but outrageous pain, suffering, isn't merely a theological problem. Outrageous pain is a failure of intimacy. It's a failure of intimacy.

Outrageous pain is a failure of intimacy.

We can be excited, like Mick Jagger can be in a rock concert, because we feel the evolutionary impulse rising in us, and we are outraged by the suffering.

We live in a world of outrageous pain, and the only response to outrageous pain is Outrageous Love.

WHAT IS OUTRAGEOUS LOVE?

We invite each other to show up not as a consumer but to participate full-on, open-hearted, blown open, wanting to change the world together and to support the best within each of us.

We live in a world of outrageous pain, wow! The only response to outrageous pain is Outrageous Love.

- Outrageous Love is not merely the love that's a strategy of the ego; it's not ordinary love.
- Outrageous Love is what Dante called the love that moves the sun and the stars.
- Outrageous Love is the allurement at the very core of the Cosmos that causes atoms to become molecules, molecules to make up the cells, and cells to become multicellular.
- Outrageous Love is what Tagore talked about, the Bengali mystic, when he said, *Love is not mere human sentiment, love is the heart of existence itself.*
- Outrageous Love is what we are calling Evolutionary Love.

When we talk about a planetary awakening in love, we're not talking about ordinary love, and we are not talking about love which is a strategy of the ego, and we are not talking about that love which won't take us home, we are talking about Evolutionary Love.

There's an enormous difference between the two. Hold someone's hand that you love with ordinary love, the strategy-of-the-ego love, your hand feels a little clammy and you want to get your hand out of there as soon as you can.

Hold someone's hand with Evolutionary Love, and the world stands still.

Pick up a baby with ordinary love, the baby keeps crying. Pick up a baby with Evolutionary Love, with Outrageous Love... wow, wow! It's a big deal. So gentle, so gentle, so gentle, so gentle.

When we talk about outrageous pain, we're actually letting in the outrageous pain of the world. We're saying that outrageous pain isn't a theological problem, it's a failure of intimacy, it's a failure to realize that we're all one. **That if someone doesn't have something to eat somewhere in the world, then we all don't have something to eat. If someone goes to sleep feeling brutalized, we all feel brutalized.**

THE GREAT QUESTION OF MEANING IS: *WHO ARE YOU?*

It's the question we all need to answer.

We want to offer what we think is the best answer based on the best understanding of all of the great traditions of Spirit, the interior sciences. All the great traditions of psychology, all the great traditions of sociology, of systems theory, of chaos theory, of complexity theory, of evolutionary science.

The greatest answer to the question of, *Who are you? Who am I? Who are we?*

Who are you?

You are an irreducibly unique expression of the LoveIntelligence and LoveBeauty that is the initiating and animating energy of All-That-Is. That lives in you, as you, and through you. That never was, is, or will be ever again, other than through you.

Wow! We stand together as expressions of Outrageous Love, expressions of Evolutionary Love. And then we realize the answer to the question of, *Who are you?*

You are an irreducibly unique expression of the LoveIntelligence and LoveBeauty of all of Reality that's telling a story in you, as you, and through you.

The Universe is having a "you experience".

And as such, you have an irreducible unique perspective, which manifests your unique capacity to give your unique gift, in your unique circle of intimacy and influence, that can be given by no one that ever was, is, or will be other than you.

You are the unique expression of Evolutionary Love that stands on the abyss of darkness and says, *Let there be light.*

With your unique frequency of light that can be articulated, expressed, and shared by no one other than you.

Do we have the right to get excited? Have we exiled excitement to fundamentalist churches? And do we call it preaching? No! We can get excited at a rock concert; we can get excited as our excitement is the excitement of evolution arising in us.

We have to feel the greatest passion possible. The passion for transformation. The passion for loving each other, for awakening as Outrageous Love, as Unique Selves in a Unique Self Symphony.

UNIQUE SELF SYMPHONY AS AN EXPRESSION OF THE SELF-ORGANIZING UNIVERSE

Unique Self Symphony is an expression of the self-organizing Universe coming together to heal, to transform, to be awake and alive in love.

We awaken as Unique Selves in a Unique Self Symphony, and we speak our voices into the Unique Self Symphony.

Unique Self Symphony begins right now: we are an irreducible expression of the entire impulse of evolution.

Teilhard de Chardin gave us the idea that when the noosphere, the mind sphere—now the internet and social media sphere—gets its collective eyes, when it is filled with enough love and awareness, it will transform the Earth into a Field of Love.

I believe what is actually true is that everybody's voice, as an expression of that irreducible impulse of evolution, when it is consciously expressed and placed into the mind sphere or internet sphere, codes itself as part of the planetary birth.

We are invited to speak our voices as a frequency of evolution entering into the mind sphere, the nervous system of humanity, as one of the millions of impulses towards the planetary awakening. **After a certain number of voices are heard in the Unique Self Symphony, resonating internally with that impulse, the planet will awaken to itself as a whole.**

We say,

This is my unique gift.

This is my unique contribution.

This is my voice.

This is what I'm standing for in Reality.

We're speaking our voices into the Unique Self Symphony, and *it matters*! The noosphere, the thinking level, the heart-essence level of Reality hears that voice, and it's recorded, that voice is recorded.

We become part of the Unique Self Symphony and the planetary awakening in love actually begins to happen.

- We are not politically correct; we are spiritually incorrect.
- We are loving each other.
- We want to love our way to enlightenment.
- We are going to enact, together, this new emergent of consciousness.
- We will respond to outrageous pain with Outrageous Love.
- We awaken as Outrageous Love as a Unique Self Symphony.

We're going to be audacious. We're going to reach as far as we can, because a man's reach, a woman's reach should exceed her grasp—or what is heaven for? Let's rock this open—so gently, so tenderly, so audaciously.

> *The blessing for all of us,*
>
> *through each of us,*
>
> *is to say yes to that impulse within you*
>
> *that is your highest expression of love and creativity,*
>
> *and let that be so.*

Amen. In the original language it means trust, it means to believe in each other. It means that **the Divine trusts us to take this new evolutionary leap, together.**

CHAPTER TWO

THE GREAT QUESTION OF MEANING: WHO ARE YOU?

Episode 2 — November 5, 2016

ACCESSING THE EVOLUTIONARY IMPULSE WITHIN

There is—within every one of us—an impulse that comes from the resonance of the universal process of creation.

When we join together, in a Field of Resonance, we often can hear that impulse more deeply in our own consciousness, and then we have the capacity to communicate that impulse with others—an impulse that awakens us to the awareness that we are part of one universal process of creation.

We are creating a shared field for every one of us to come alive with the consciousness of evolution within us, to attune internally to the most profound resonance of the Divine within us.

In the early Christian religion, they spoke of the second coming of Christ, a total awakening of something radically new. In this resonant field, every one of us is coming into a radical new being of personhood as a contribution to a new planetary consciousness bringing in the Divine process of creation in every one of us. Each one of us is contributing our unique Field of Resonance at the exact time on the planet when the planetary body, the organism of which we are all cells, is awakening collectively. There is no more awesome potential than this.

This is a pivotal moment, a historic moment. We are seeking to evolve church, synagogue, mosque, temple, and zendo.

PRAYER: GOD LIVES BOTH IN US AND HOLDS US

- ◆ We are seeking to participate together in the very evolution of what prayer means.
- ◆ We are not talking about the old vision of prayer.
- ◆ We are talking about evolutionary prayer.

We are talking about the evolutionary God in which we both bow and participate together in the very evolution of God. We are pouring new evolutionary wine into old flasks, which is the way of evolution itself. When we talk about God, we first say, *the god you don't believe in doesn't exist.*

Prayer now means something greater, larger, deeper.

What is the experience of prayer? The experience of prayer is knowing:

- ◆ That Reality hears us.
- ◆ That when we speak, Reality—which is sometimes called God by the mystics (God and Reality are the same)—All-That-Is hears.
- ◆ Our words are not spoken into a vacuum.

This is a pointing-out instruction.

The phrase, pointing-out instruction, we borrowed from our Tibetan Buddhist friends. A pointing-out instruction means we point to something that we already know. What do we already know?

For instance, we already know that we can hear each other talk. Not just through the physical structure of the ear but we can actually hear through the intelligence that animates our uniqueness. And, we each participate in the larger intelligence of Cosmos. We are each a *part* of the loving intelligence of Reality.

That's what prayer means:

- Reality knows my name.
- We live in an Intimate Universe.
- God is not merely the Infinity of Power, which all the great traditions talked about so eloquently, but God is, if you will, the Infinity of Intimacy.

God is the Infinity of Intimacy.

When we have an intimate, emotional relationship then that intimacy participates in the larger intimacy of Cosmos.

And we can realize that, wherever we fall, we fall into divine intimacy—we fall into God's hands.

Not as a fundamentalist statement, in which we abandon ourselves, but *we*, as what Dante called *divine miniatures*, baby-faced divines, are unique expressions of the evolutionary impulse that lives alive and awake in us.

Wow! To know that:

- we are held,
- the Universe intends us,
- the Universe recognizes us,
- the Universe knows our name,
- God is the Infinity of Intimacy.

When we fall down on our knees in prayer, we turn to the most personal intimate source of all of Reality, the infinite personhood of Reality, and we say:

> *Help me.*
>
> *Help me be the best that you need me to be!*

Help my uncle, and my friend.

Help my physical body.

Help Reality.

Help there be peace on Earth.

Help my sister get through the difficult moment in her marriage.

Help me find the strength and the capacity to transform.

We pray to the God who is the Infinity of Intimacy and the Infinity of Power, of which we are not separate—and yet which holds us in the very same moment.

We are relieved. We get to return to prayer at a higher level of consciousness, not as obedient slaves but as *divine miniatures.* We are madly in love with the Divine that birthed us, that intended us, that knows our name.

Because remember, the loving, intelligent Cosmos manifested mitosis and meiosis and photosynthesis, all before there was ever a human neocortex, all before there was ever a supercomputer.

Reality intends us, is us, and holds us.

We turn to God, to the Infinity of Intimacy, in whose hands we can allow ourselves to be held, in whose arms we can fall. We fall on our knees in devotion, filled with the audacity of our devotion, and we ask for everything.

We ask for everything because prayer affirms the dignity of personal need. We are reclaiming prayer on the evolutionary path. We are loosening the grips of our brothers and sisters, our holy brothers and sisters, the fundamentalists—and we love them dearly—who say, *prayer is only to my God, who only knows me and my people and no other people.* We say no to that!

We say, *God both lives in all of us and holds all of us.*

The god you don't believe in doesn't exist, and we fall on our knees to pray to the God who is the Infinity of Intimacy, and in this, we reclaim evolutionary intimacy with each other. We pray. We bow our heads in prayer in the delight of knowing that we are held.

Smolo tachat roshi: His left hand is under my head.

Viymino t'chabkeni: His right hand embraces me.

Every place we fall, we fall into the arms of the Evolutionary God.

We offer up a prayer in song. Our hymn book is songs that find their way into culture, that express a prayer that we all want and yearn for so deeply. Because we are about Evolutionary Love, Outrageous Love.

So, let's offer up a prayer for *knowing what love is*, and we enter meditation now: "I Want to Know What Love Is" [*see appendix*].

PLANETARY AWAKENING THROUGH UNIQUE SELF SYMPHONY

- ◆ We set our intention to play a larger game.
- ◆ We set our intention to participate in the evolution of love.
- ◆ **We set our intention to awaken as evolutionary lovers, to love the moment open, and to usher in heaven on Earth**.

We feel so connected to everybody; we feel full of a planetary awakening right now. *This* is how the planet awakens.

It is not something that's going to happen years in the future. You know why? *We* plan it. That is to say, every human being awakening *is* the planetary awakening. Isn't that true? It is not just something in the future.

We have been drawn together through the eons of time, because we were given a frequency internally. It is like an inner impulse of creation. It must be like what David Bohm called the *implicate order of evolution* that came from the origin of creation, that turns you on to a specific frequency of purpose.

More than *my life's purpose*—it seems to me to be literally a Field of Consciousness in every being. It is from the pattern of creation that originated in the Big Bang. It set the billions of years going. The calling right now is the pattern, the frequency, the feeling of the vibrational field *in you*. It is vibrating with a frequency that is both a universal source of creation and going in the direction of the story of evolution.

Our frequency—in its origin—comes from the impulse that created what we call a Cosmic Love Story, that has attracted quark with quark, electron with electron, and cell with cell for billions and billions of years.

Through love.

Through attraction.

To ever more complex systems.

Ever more creative, ever more free to win or lose, destroy or create.

Ever more capable of conscious connection with the source within us, directed toward the next stage of evolution.

Tune into the experiential frequency that motivates you at the very, very heart of your soul—**what are you born to do?**

You did not make it up—it made *you* up.

You did not create it—it created *you*.

When you tune into this vibrational universal intelligent field, there is a feeling in there.

- ◆ It is the feeling somehow God is within, vibrating with the unique aspect of my being.
- ◆ It is a fusion with the Godhead, that is to say, the inner impulse of my own frequency and passion.
- ◆ It feels that it is coming from Source, blending with divine energy.

THE UNIVERSE IS ORCHESTRATING A SYMPHONY OF FREQUENCIES

We've chosen to do this, we are part of a larger frequency. It comes from the source of creation, but it comes in *as each person's uniqueness*. The Universe is orchestrating a symphony of frequencies. This is true.

We are challenged to nurture an environment expecting the radical transformation of humanity into a co-creative species, one with the Divine.

Everywhere on Earth, anyone, anywhere, who feels this frequency, this is omnipresent universally. This is not a frequency that is made up. Teilhard de Chardin said that when the noosphere— the thinking layer of Earth—is filled with the vibrational voices, sounds, or feelings of people in love, the entire nervous system of humanity awakens.

We don't know how many impulses are required for the nervous system of a planetary body—which is, you might call it, a newborn planetary culture—to awaken humanity.

However, we are going to make our contribution toward it. **We are going to hold an expectation that everybody's impulse is vital. It cannot be done without you. It cannot awaken without you.** The Universe really likes us to do this together. I just know that. That's my clue.

How many frequencies does it take? How many people on Earth would like to contribute to that frequency?

Reach out and reach in, into Source and out toward everybody on Earth, so that *union* occurs. There is a degree of shared awakening that only the mystics of the human race have ever experienced before. While we are struggling with all the birth crises of energy, fighting each other, **we are also the birth of the emerging species.**

Our theme is *evolutionary intimacy*.

We are going to have practices.

We are going to have shared experiences.

We are going to become a new community on Earth.

THE PRACTICE OF EVOLUTIONARY CHANT

We are laying down tracks: a new vision of the Evolutionary God, a new vision of *Planetary Awakening in Love through Unique Self Symphonies.*

We are reclaiming prayer. Let us also reclaim *chant.* Let us reintroduce the practice of chant. Let us do chants from different traditions, different fields of rock music, and different fields of classical music, and different great traditions.

Our first chant is *Om Nama Shivaya, Hallelujah.* A great chant from Kashmir Shaivism, from our Hindu brothers and sisters. [*See appendix.*]

Om Nama Shivaya means, I greet you.

Shiva means the Reality principle, the great evolutionary principle of Reality.

Hallelujah means *Holelut.*

Hallel—ecstatic praise.

I breathe in.

Yah is the very breath of life.

So, *Hallelujah* is the ecstatic praise of the breath of life that lives through us.

Om Nama Shivaya, Hallelujah.

Always chant from the heart. Don't worry about your voice. That which comes from the heart enters the heart.

Om Nama Shivaya. Hey, Om Nama Shivaya. Hallelujah.
Om Nama Shivaya. Hey, Om Nama Shivaya. Hallelujah.
Om Nama Shivaya. Hey, Om Nama Shivaya. Hallelujah.

Om Nama Shivaya. Hey, Om Nama Shivaya. Hallelujah.

And, we rest in the aftertaste, the secret always rests in the aftertaste.

We chant because we realize: the Universe feels, and the Universe feels love.

To really get that: *the Universe feels love.*

That is not merely a spiritual idea. That the Universe feels is the best scientific understanding of Reality that we have today in both the exterior sciences and the interior sciences.

Evolution is driven by an evolutionary Eros, an Evolutionary Love.

- What Dante called the love that moved the sun and other stars.
- What Alfred North Whitehead called the movement of Reality through the gentle persuasion of love towards love.
- What Tagore, the Bengali mystic meant when he said, love is not mere human sentiment. Love is the heart of existence itself.

It's to really know that we are loved by the Universe.

But, not in a kind of fundamentalist way, like I'm not worthy, and I'm loved even though I'm not worthy because I'm obedient. No, no, no. We are each loved because we are each infinitely worthy. We have infinite adequacy, and infinite dignity.

To actually know: I'm a desired child of the Universe.

Just feel into that sentence: I'm a desired child of the Universe.

And here's another chant that speaks from Libby Roderick. Everyone will get it. "How Could Anyone?" [*See appendix.*]

Write the name of a person that you might like to sing this to. Just by writing the name of that person, they're in the chant. *How could anyone ever tell you that you are anything less than beautiful? How could anyone ever tell you...* just write the name, and they'll hear it. *That you are less than whole?* Write the names.

How can anyone fail to notice that our love, that our love is just a miracle. And how deeply we are connected in our souls.

WE ARE OUTRAGEOUS LOVERS

We are Outrageous Lovers. Outrageous Love is the heart of existence itself, and we're not embarrassed to love each other. Ordinary love is love which is the strategy of the ego. We're not embarrassed to be Rumi. We're not embarrassed to be ecstatic; we're not embarrassed to be in devotion. We don't consider devotion co-dependent. No, we're *interdependent.* We love each other madly.

When we say Planetary Awakening through Unique Self Symphonies, we just need to ask one question which is the great question of meaning, of science, and of spirit. *Who are you? Who are you?*

There's only one answer to this question.

It's based on the best integration of traditional, modern, postmodern, and post-postmodern thought

It's based on integrating chaos theory, and complexity theory, and evolutionary science, and all the schools of psychology and anthropology, and different forms of physics, and biology, and sacred numerology—all of it together.

This is the answer, and it's so gorgeous.

Who are you?

You are an irreducibly unique expression of the *LoveIntelligence* and *Love-Beauty,*that is the initiating, animating energy and Eros of All-That-Is,that lives in you, as you, and through you, that never was, is, or will be ever again, other than through you.

You embody and incarnate a unique quality of intimacy in the Infinity of Intimacy.

You hold a unique perspective, which manifests your unique capacity to give your unique gift within your unique circle of intimacy and influence, to address a unique need in Reality that can be addressed by you and you alone.

If you fall asleep while on the watch of your life, if you don't awaken to the full power of your irreducible, unique gorgeousness, and your irreducible, unique quality of intimacy, then there is a corner of the world unloved because you have not yet stood on the abyss of darkness and said let there be light.

CONFESSIONS OF GREATNESS

For a moment, realize that your voice is the frequency of the Universe. The vibrational quality of voice, in the beginning, was the word. The word is made flesh. When the word is spoken, with a vibrational frequency of the unique essence of your being, it actually is translated into form.

All the great words of history, whether it be the New Testament or the various sacred texts, or the writings of Plato, if they were not written down and spoken in words, it would not have been enough just to have thought them.

In your voice, as you speak, is the vibrational field of your unique essence becoming a word. You put your attention on the frequency of vibration of the impulse that is that word.

You're invited to say these words out loud: *I am an expression of divine intent. I am confessing my greatness, which is God's greatness, as me.*

When we confess our greatness, it's not a personal egoic statement. It's daring to say yes to God.

By being able to say yes to God within you, in a word that can be heard, what happens is it actually activates the internal Reality of that within you through the vibration of your voice. And then through the larger nervous system, the noosphere is picking up the vibration of your voice.

So let's hear if it can vibrate from the impulse of the Divine *as* your greatness. It is not about what is better than others about you but about what is God in you speaking.

I'll start: *I am intent for planetary awakening, that the love and genius in each of us will be shared, in a symphony so magnificent that the world will be awakened to the next stage of evolution. That is the God in me, God's greatness through me.*

Speak God's greatness through you for a moment.

For instance, *I am Outrageous Love, keeping every boundary that should be kept, and breaking every boundary of smallness and contraction, to honor in devotion every unique voice in the Unique Self Symphony.*

Everybody is here because of this impulse of creation within you.

REALITY IS AN OUTRAGEOUS LOVE STORY

Where are we?

We are in a planetary awakening.

Who are we?

We are evolving God. We are evolving prayer. We are evolving love.

What do we know?

We are the leading edge. We are the people who say that we realize that Reality is not a fact; Reality is a story. That's what evolution teaches us. Reality is not merely an internal fact, as even Einstein thought; Reality is a story. *Reality is a story* means that it's going somewhere, and we are personally implicated in the story.

What else do we know?

The good news that Reality is not really a fact; it's a story. But it's not an ordinary story. Reality is a love story. Reality is an Evolutionary Love Story.

We have scripture on this, and it's the scripture of all the great traditions, and all the evolutionary sciences, and all the wisdom traditions integrated into this larger integral embrace.

That's not a poetic idea, nor a saccharine, nor a New Age, nor a religious idea; **it's the best take we have of Reality at this moment in time. Reality is not just a story. Reality is a love story. Reality is not an ordinary love story; it's an Outrageous Love Story.**

It's evolutionary Eros and Evolutionary Love that drives the entire story.

Because *the Universe: A Love Story* is an Intimate Universe, and social synergy is an expression of that Intimate Universe that we want to unfold this new evolution of the very source code of culture and consciousness through.

Thank you, Universe, for allowing us to explore and be this together, *Amen.*

CHAPTER THREE

A WORLD INFUSED WITH EVOLUTIONARY LOVE

Episode 3 — November 12, 2016

METAMORPHOSIS FROM *HOMO SAPIENS* TO *HOMO AMOR*

Imagine looking at Earth from space. See what the astronauts see. Be a universal being, free of the Earth.

See the mystery, the story revealed as an evolutionary process of creation from nothing at all, to everything that was, is, and will be through you, now, today.

You were there before the Big Bang. You are consciousness created. You are source sourcing. If you have seen yourself, you have seen the Creator within. You and the Creator are one.

We are undergoing a metamorphosis from *Homo sapiens*—the creature that knows that it knows itself as separate from each other and nature— to *Homo Amor*, the being who embodies the process of creation uniquely as you.

As your own passion to love more, create more, evolve more, you are embodying the impulse of creation itself. You, and I, and we, are evolution becoming conscious of itself as us. Every thought, every action, is evolutionary.

Breathe. Now. From the source of creation. From the mind of God. In our resonant field. Just place your attention on the source of creation.

Just breathe it up, the entire evolutionary spiral into your own being. You and I are expressions of the source of creation. Open your evolutionary eyes now, and see the light as a new human, an evolving human, who is becoming one with nature and one with source.

Take the new context, which gives you the capacity for evolutionary eyes, which reveals to you the mystery story of creation, and is able to see yourself and be yourself with evolutionary eyes, heart, mind, and intuition. See yourself as a natural Christ.

Love God above all else.

Love your nature as yourself and all of nature as yourself. Love yourself as a natural Christ, capable of loving, and being, and doing the miracle, yourself.

Combined with science and technology, we are all being changed. We are combining Christ, Buddha, spirituality, Krishna, and love, with the new technologies of creation to become *Homo amor*. Feeling the Earth. Freeing the people. Exploring the vast reaches of the human mind and the planet beyond us.

Evolve yourself now.

All of us, in whom the flame of expectation burns, to become Outrageous Lovers, doing our unique work to evolve ourselves within this world.

We are here to bring the divine impulse of love, to evolutionize politics with love.

FROM A FUNDAMENTALIST GOD TO AN EVOLUTIONARY GOD

We are in the Evolutionary Church.

We are up-leveling and evolving the consciousness of what it means when we say the word church.

We are up-leveling and evolving the consciousness of what it means when we say God.

Evolutionary Church and evolutionary God.

- God as the personal force.
- God as the impersonal force, animating the evolutionary impulse.
- God as the ceaseless creativity of the Cosmos, birthing ever greater levels of recognition, union, and embrace.
- God that lives in us, as us, and through us, as the irreducible, unique expression of that love and intelligence, which is God.
- God that holds us even as God is us.

In that paradox, have you ever read Rumi? Rumi is always holding that paradox. Rumi is always the friend. Rumi is always aflame with LoveIntelligence, the Divinity of all that is bursting as Rumi, even as Rumi falls into the arms of God at the same time.

One of the great evolutions of consciousness—calling all of us—is the reclaiming of God.

The liberation of the word God from the grasp of fundamentalism to an evolutionary God, where we actually experience the personal force of Cosmos that lives in us, holding us, is essential.

Feel into that possibility. Feel into this notion of evolutionary prayer. What is evolutionary prayer?

Evolutionary prayer is the ability to know that when we talk, Reality hears us. The personal force in each of us hears each other talk. When we talk, Reality hears us.

So, our speech is a prayer. It's not just that we hear each other, but the intelligence that lives in each of us, the personal intelligence, which is our uniqueness of Cosmos, participates in the larger LoveIntelligence of Reality that hears our words, that holds us.

We realize *every time we fall, we fall into God's hands.* **Every time we fall, we fall into the LoveIntelligence of Reality that intended my existence.**

And that is what we mean by evolutionary prayer.

EVOLUTIONARY PRAYER: THE INFINITE FORCE OF COSMOS KNOWS YOUR NAME

Here is a wild story, a story about a great master, Levy Isaac. When Levy Isaac would try to make a blessing—and the blessing in Hebrew is *baruch atah,* which means blessed are you, God, *melech ha-olam,* king, queen of the world.

Levy Isaac would begin to make the blessing, and he would say:

> *Blessed are you.*
>
> *You...*
>
> *You...*
>
> *You!*
>
> *YOU!!!*

And he would faint in ecstasy.

Wow! What did he mean?

Levy Isaac wasn't a primitive regressive. He didn't believe in a kind of fundamentalist vision of reality. Levy Isaac was a great, non-dual evolutionary mystic.

What he said was, *You. You. You!*

What does that mean?

It means when he would make a blessing, he would feel the *You*. He would feel the presence of the infinite, personal LoveIntelligence that knew his name.

Imagine, Barack Obama is still president. Imagine if you received a phone call from Barack Obama, and Barack says:

> *I've been watching you for the last 30 years.*
>
> *I know everything about you.*
>
> *I know your childhood. I know your thoughts. I know your dreams.*
>
> *You have something that we need here in the United States of America.*
>
> *And no one else has it but you.*
>
> *And I just want you to know, I'm right here with you.*
>
> *I've never been anywhere else. I've been holding you.*
>
> *I'm madly in love with you.*
>
> *We each are utterly needed by all of Reality.*

It took 13.7 billion years to manifest synchronicities that would birth the unique cellular pattern of each of us, the unique DNA structure, the unique subatomic, molecular structure.

Let us step into prayer, with an evolutionary prayer meditation.

Imagine the infinite force of the Cosmos.

As we shut our eyes,

- ♦ Imagine the photons.

- Imagine all the hadrons from quarks.
- Imagine the entire molecular structure of Reality.
- Imagine the infinite force of Reality intensifying, birthing every stage of evolution.
- Imagine the complexity of all the chemical structures, the magnificence of mitosis, meiosis, and photosynthesis.
- Imagine the most gorgeous, stunning, dazzling complexity, barely, barely glimpsed by all of the sciences.

Beauty. Brilliance. Infinite power beyond imagination. Spanning across billions and billions of light years. Eons and eons of time. An incandescent, ephemeral, and yet eternal, dazzling, complex, brilliant, loving, beauty of force, of power beyond imagination.

We call this God in the third person: the God of physics, chemistry, and power.

The impersonal everything that moves through the Cosmos. Unimaginable. Way beyond anything we can even begin to grasp.

Imagine all of that, all of that infinite, gorgeous power, sitting in a chair, looking at you with the most kind, tender eyes and saying:

I love you so much.

I need you.

I know you.

You've felt intimate in your life?

Well, I am the source of all that intimacy. I am the Infinity of Intimacy and the Infinity of Power, sitting in a chair right next to you, knowing your name.

That's the experience of prayer. To know that every place we fall, we fall into God's hands.

The God you don't believe in doesn't exist. Not the fundamentalist God.

But the God who is infinitely personal, the God who is the Infinity of Intimacy, the God who knows everything about you, the God who intended your existence, the God who invites you to participate in and as God, before *that* God, we offer prayer.

That God says to us: *Ask for everything.*

That God says to us that when you pray, you affirm the dignity of your personal need because prayer affirms the dignity of personal need.

So friends, beloveds, all of us who stand in the presence of the Divine. Even as God invites us to be God, God holds us as God. So, we're going to pray to God. Now, we're going to pray and ask for everything.

I want to ask everyone to just write your prayer, whatever your prayer is. Speak it out loud.

> *I want to ask for my mother, who lives in the Middle East, to be healthy, and her husband, David, who's 93, to be well.*
>
> *Opening the intimate chambers of my heart.*
>
> *I pray for my own health and my own vitality.*
>
> *I pray for Barbara's gorgeous health and that she will be with us for many, many years, shining her radiance.*
>
> *I pray for funds for the planetary mission.*
>
> *I pray for my uncle Max, who's in the hospital doing cancer treatment, to be well.*

We offer our prayer, and we ask for everything.

Because we are dignified.

Because we matter before God.

Because we are the Divine intention.

In this moment of prayer. In the Field of Resonance.

The heavens open. The heavens that live in us. The heavens that are the evolutionary Personhood of all of Reality.

Yes. Yes. We offer our prayers. As we offer prayer, our field of prayer comes together. **We offer personal prayer, and we offer prayer for the people that matter to us. Then we extend our field, and we pray for all, and they're both critical.**

> *I pray for infinite abundance for all beings on Earth.*
>
> *I pray for the funds and time for the writing that I need to do.*
>
> *I pray to live my purpose fully.*
>
> *Lord, fill the void with peace and harmony.*
>
> *I pray for my partner and to find success, to be able to live together in love.*
>
> *I pray for the good health of my mother, sister, and myself.*
>
> *I pray for the youth of America and the world.*

Take a risk, take a risk, and pray. We thought we'd abandoned prayer. We thought we'd lost God. We thought that only the god that we don't believe in owns the space of God, and we're here to evolve God. God invites us to participate in the evolution of God and to reclaim prayer at a higher level of consciousness.

We offer our chant prayer, "How Could Anyone?" [*See appendix.*]

A POLITICS OF EVOLUTIONARY LOVE

Our theme for this week is evolutionary politics, a politics of Evolutionary Love.

In this week, in which President-elect Donald Trump stepped into the scene, in which half of the country is ecstatic in the United States of America, and half of the country is in mourning, the world watches with great uncertainty.

We live at a time when the impossible happens. There's this intensifying disorder. All that we thought was regular and normal is suspended and bracketed; the very institutions which we thought we understood are acting in ways in which they've always acted underneath the surface but we've ignored it. There's this break out of the unexpected, of disorder.

And this new space emerges, the space in between the stories.

The old story no longer applies, and yet the new story is not quite written. This is the space in between.

We have scripture on this. The *Book of Numbers* says: *And the voice of God speaks in the arc of the covenant, from the space in between the cherubs. Bein ha-kruvim*, in the original Hebrew.

In the space in between, in the cracks in between—which is where we are today, the space in between stories—a new story can emerge. We articulate for Reality, in this space in between the stories, a new politics of love, a new evolutionary politics of love. What does that mean, not as a New Age idea, but as a genuine structure for the next stage in evolution?

Clearly, we have a choice. We're either going to regress, or we're going to evolve. We're either going to go backward, or we're going to actually leap to a higher level of consciousness.

Our crisis is a birth.

We're at a moment of crisis, at which either we'll go backwards in the worst of ways, or we'll evolve in the best of ways, because we live in the best of times, and we live in the worst of times.

FROM PARLIAMENTARY PROCEDURE TO A POLITICS OF EVOLUTIONARY LOVE

The first tenant of the evolutionary politics of love is the awareness that **everyone on Earth is nothing less than beautiful**. And that is because

Source created all of us. No matter what the divisions. No matter what the differences that come mainly from the separated mind.

The second thing that is **the basis of evolutionary politics is the fact that we, as a planet, are shifting to the next stage of evolution.** This means that every single person, no matter where they come from or what their inner politics are, is part of a planetary crisis of birth, of the next stage of evolution—or devolution and possible extinction of Earth life.

Everybody. Regardless of politics.

Another thing about evolutionary politics is that there is a time frame. Do we have hundreds of years to make the change?

We do not.

In that sense, the crisis is truly like a birth. A baby grows relatively peacefully in the womb for nine months. And then something appallingly challenging occurs to the baby. It's dislodged from its past. It's forced into a frightening canal. It comes out impotent for the first second. It doesn't like it.

Most of us are still in that first second, just after the planet has actually integrated itself into a whole system—with a nervous system, connecting hundreds of us, if not all of us. Connected. We're born in that but we're still shocked.

Oh my god. I don't know how to do this. I used to be so good. Now, I don't know. My system is dying out.

You could have 1,000 different problems because you're living at the next stage of social evolution. However, if you have evolutionary eyes, if you have taken an overview perspective, if you have the capacity to understand *gestalt*—our whole system patterns—then you will see that **while the pain is increasing on planet Earth in many ways, it is also increasing in capability, in awakened consciousness, in social caring, in high technologies giving us powers we used to attribute to the gods.**

Now consider this:

- Evolutionary politics is growing up out of evolutionary humans.
- It is growing up like the people who are reading this book.
- It's growing up out of those of us who feel the impulse of evolution, who've seen breakdowns of five mass extinctions before we got here, seen billions of species extinct before we got here.

We see ourselves as the very first species ever on Earth to be aware of evolution, to be aware that we are affecting it by everything that we do, that **we have moved from evolution by chance to evolution by choice.**

We recognize that the source of the choices we make as evolutionaries comes from the impulse of evolution itself.

Evolution made a radical choice at the beginning. It set a radical intention for greater consciousness, greater freedom, more complex and loving order in every new turn on the spiral.

Those of us interested and able to create an evolutionary politics are seeing us at the exact moment of the breakdown.

What's really breaking *down* is the illusion of separation. What's breaking *through* is something new. We're calling it *evolutionary politics.*

Just taking a moment to realize,

- Democracy was a huge advance over monarchy. In monarchy, you had no identity. The queen could boil you in oil if she didn't like you. She could hang you in the public square, and you had no recourse.
- Out of monarchy came parliamentary procedure, win/ lose voting, a huge advance over monarchy, giving every individual the idea they could vote. It's completely radically new, empowering the individual.
- Democracy has carried the best and most fertile nations

in the world, right up to this moment, when it seems to be failing almost everywhere.

◆ Win/lose democracy is failing, because the structure makes it impossible to aim at the level of social creativity and cooperation which is needed to survive. It makes the United States of America suffer through the failure of win/lose democracy. Nobody can win in that structure. In some respects, because of that, everyone is less than who we are.

◆ So out of parliamentary procedure is a whole new procedure arising, which we happen to be doing, many of us, unconsciously. We are moving from parliamentary procedure and win/lose voting, to synergistic procedure, synergistic rules of order, in which we look for common goals. We match our needs with other people's resources in the light of the vast, new, high-tech genius of humanity, that makes it possible to do just about all the miracles that Jesus did, from resurrection to producing in abundance, to overcoming even the limits of animal/human existence.

◆ In order to begin to place our intelligence in silicon, to begin to explore beyond the planet, to sense those planets with other life, to become universal, to have a nervous system that is just awakening, like the nervous system of a newborn child. This is the origin of evolutionary politics.

In order to have evolutionary politics, we have declared the introduction of a new context in which evolutionary politics takes place. We're calling it a planetary mission.

The mission is to connect co-creators worldwide in synergistic convergence, wherever they are. It is attracting, and will attract on a global scale, anyone in whom the impulse of evolution is prevailing, who wishes to be more, love more, connect more, and create more.

The evolutionary mission is simply a context for us to realize that the new politics of Evolutionary Love has a huge impact on the living nervous system, the noosphere of the planetary body.

Everything that anyone is doing is leading to:

- More co-creation
- More synergy
- More love
- More wholeness
- More oneness
- More goodness

We're calling this the *Office for the Future*, and this can be found at www.officeforthefuture.org.

- You learn synergistic decision making.
- You learn to come from the heart.
- You learn to connect with each other out of supra-sexual joy to create.

Evolutionary politics is the politics of love—to create and to join with each other to create.

This power is as intrinsic to humans as the power to join genes to have the baby.

The power of evolutionary politics is the yearning to join genius, to join creativity, to join each other in synergy, which becomes what Pierre Teilhard de Chardin calls, *higher level order or love.*

This is our moment, and our time has come.

This is the purpose: to gather the co-creators in love worldwide and shift the Field of Love from fear to co-creation.

A POLITICS OF EVOLUTIONARY LOVE IS A POLITICS OF UNIQUE SELF SYMPHONY

Amen. Amen. Hallelujah. Hallelujah. And we return, *Hallelujah.*

Hallelujah means, *hallel*—radical praise, *holelut*—intoxication, *Yah* is the name of God. *Yah* is the outbreath. We breathe in. *Yaaah*, is the outbreath. So *Hallelujah* is the ecstasy of the outbreath, the intoxication with Reality, to be God intoxicated, to be love intoxicated.

We're going to offer this to our President-elect Trump. We will be sending this to President Trump through people that we know that are related to the president and offering this vision. And this vision is a vision that all of us need to engage.

I want you to feel the part of you that says, as I say we're going to offer this to President Trump, *He's never going to listen...*, and the other part of us that says, *well, he was elected by people who are misogynist, and racist, and all the terrible people.* But actually, that would be a precise failure of love, because love at its core is empathy.

The core of love is empathy, and empathy means I can feel you. I feel how you feel.

Hate means I can't feel how you feel. I can't sense your reality.

When I'm able to ask, *What is it like to be you*, then I can feel you.

When I demonize Trump, or I demonize Trump supporters, I don't actually hold the complexity. Why would someone vote for Donald Trump? Our assumption is they must be misogynist, bigoted, racist, terrible human beings. Wrong. That's the first failure of love.

People voted for Trump for many reasons. Some of them were misogynistic. Some of them were racist but that's not what the core of it was. Even when there is misogyny and racism, even when there is hate and fear, you have to find out what's underneath the fear. What's underneath the hate. You know?

When people get lost in hate, that means they're covering something up. **Hate is just a cover. It's body armor for pain. Hate is body armor for grief, for sadness.**

And when people liberate themselves from hate, they're forced to deal with the pain, which is why they don't want to be liberated.

Let's all realize we are all in this together. On this spaceship Earth. There's no place to hide. And that which unites us is so much greater than that which divides us.

Let's try and articulate together with passion, with delight, the tenets of a politics of Evolutionary Love. Emergent from all of the beautiful visions we lay out with so much grace, and inspiration, and dignity that moves through all of us.

A POLITICS OF EVOLUTIONARY LOVE IS A POLITICS OF EVOLUTIONARY INTIMACY

We introduce a really simple idea: We live in a world of outrageous pain. The only response to outrageous pain is Outrageous Love.

Sometimes we hear, *Wow, we really get that,* but other times people say, *Why are you talking about pain? That's a downer. Let's uplift this.*

But, actually, there's no bypass.

- ◆ When we're not able to understand the pain of a father who's been laid off from his manufacturing job, who can't afford to pay child support, who's lost his connection to what it means to be a man. And there are millions and millions of American men like that. When we can't access men who feel degraded and debased, because the very image of the masculine has

47

been degraded and debased.

- When we can't understand the pain of the feminine, that feels like, I don't have a place to be radiant, I can't shine without being reduced and objectified, I want to fully own my radiance and offer it as a gift, but I don't feel like there's a masculinity that can receive it.
- When we don't understand the pain of millions of people who go to sleep at night alone, in lonely desperation.
- When we don't understand the millions and millions of people who are not sure how to pay the rent this month, not sure how to put food on the table this month. And those people live among us. And sometimes they even hide it from us, because they feel ashamed.
- When we forget the places when we were radically vulnerable. When we forget the places when we were radically dependent, and we hold the illusion of our autonomy, the illusion of our independence. When we don't feel together with our outrageous beauty, our outrageous fragility.

When I can't feel you, when you don't feel me feeling you, then there's a violation of intimacy. A politics of Evolutionary Love is a politics of evolutionary intimacy.

Intimacy means I feel you, and you feel me, and I feel you feeling me, and you feel me feeling you. You get that? Intimacy means we feel each other, and we feel each other feeling each other. When that happens, something new emerges. A new possibility is born. Because God is nothing if not the possibility of possibility.

So, what is the politics of Evolutionary Love?

A politics of Evolutionary Love, a politics of Outrageous Love, says every human being is an irreducible, Unique Self with a unique gift to give to our brothers, our sisters, our beloveds, our friends, our family, and a unique gift to give into the larger *evolutionary field*.

Every person's not just a Unique Self, an irreducibly unique expression of the LoveIntelligence, but every person is an Evolutionary Unique Self. Every person is intended by All-That-Is. Every person is needed by All-That-Is.

There's no one outside the circle.

We talk about hatred spewed in the conservative media and the Trump camps. I want to tell you something that's hard to hear. You know, **there's just as much hatred in the liberal world. But the hatred is hidden, it's dressed up in pretty phrases. It's the hatred of** *other,* **the dismissal, the refusal to feel the place of** *other*, **the refusal to access genuine compassion that allows one to feel empathy for those who are outside of their camp.**

The amount of people that I know, that you know, that don't know anyone who voted for Trump, how is that possible? Actually, there are people all around you who voted for Trump who didn't tell you. Ask all sorts of people you're interacting with in your life. Maybe you were at a hotel and it was the woman who changed the sheets, who felt desperate, because they could never actually move in the social scale, because they were locked in and not taken care of. And they felt that no one was feeling their oppression. And for whatever reason, Donald Trump was able to access that feeling and say, *I'm gonna rebuild America again.*

It doesn't matter whether you feel it yourself or not. It doesn't matter whether you feel or not feel the Donald. We all know the critique. We all know the critique with Donald Trump. The critique is real, and it's powerful, and it's devastating. And wow, **if I can't access that in me which would vote for Trump, if I can't access that part in me that would cast that ballot, then I've projected all of the stuff onto someone else, the** *other*, **the demon.**

We have to get underneath that. **We have to feel into the part of ourselves that's going to vote for Donald Trump. When we do that, then empathy opens up.**

UNIQUE SELVES COME TOGETHER IN A UNIQUE SELF SYMPHONY

A politics of Evolutionary Love is a politics of Unique Self Symphony.

It's a key idea in evolutionary science. We live in a self-organizing Universe. Meaning there's an inherent principle in Reality which self-organizes. Desiring more love. And more good. And more consciousness. And more giving. And more presence.

- ◆ That's the principle that governs an ant hill. Telling every ant, so every ant knows what to do, because pheromones are secreted, and the ants come together and form this gorgeous, self-organizing universe.
- ◆ In the human world, it's the same thing. We self-organize. How do we self-organize? We self-organize if we access in ourselves the pheromone, the interior chemical, which is the unique expression of LoveIntelligence that is my Unique Self, that's the unique allurement of my life.
- ◆ When we let ourselves be drawn by our unique allurement, when we let ourselves be drawn to commit our outrageous acts of love in unison with each other, and we begin to play our instrument in the Unique Self Symphony, we stop having a top-down government. We stop having a top-down corporation. We stop having a top-down society.
- ◆ We begin to have a bottom-up, self-organizing politics, a bottom-up, self-organizing activism, a bottom-up, self-organizing love, a bottom-up, self-organizing empathy.
- ◆ **We unleash a power, a potential, a potency through this self-organization that has more capacity to heal, to transform, than all the corporations and all the governments together. The government itself becomes self-organizing.**
- ◆ No Unique Self is left out of the circle. We hold a shared vision.

We tell you something shocking. Donald Trump is a lover. Does it get distorted? Yes, it does. But at his core, Donald Trump is just like you and me. Donald Trump loves his kids. He loves the United States, and we need to work with him to clarify the prism of that love.

We need to work with him because he has become the president. And we cherish, as Hillary Clinton said, we cherish the peaceful transition of power, and we need to open our hearts and say:

We're going to protest when we need to protest, and we're going to create the potency of an evolutionary politics of love. We're going to articulate a new vision.

We're going to put it together, and it's going to come when we speak it out loud.

CHAPTER FOUR

EFFECTING A PLANETARY AWAKENING: A POLITICS OF EVOLUTIONARY LOVE

Episode 4 — November 19, 2016

LET'S BE DEMONSTRATIONS OF OUR OWN CONSCIOUS EVOLUTION

Here's heart of the matter: to come from Spirit at this depth, to evolve ourselves, and to evolve our world. There are no greater impulses than exactly these.

Many years ago, I heard these words in a mystical experience: *do not abandon my church, but evolve my church into a new vehicle for new beings, and for the evolution of the body politic.*

In resonance, we are gathered here together to evolve the church, to form a new gathering of pioneering souls worldwide, who hold within ourselves:

- The impulse of the living Christ
- The impulse of the living divine
- The awakening of the new human within ourselves
- The expression of the divine intent of universal evolution for

greater consciousness, freedom, and loving order

Jesus told us, *You will do the works that I did and even greater works will you do in the fullness of time because I go to the Father.*

What does that mean? Who is the Father? Who is the Mother? **The source of creation within you, evolving you, uniquely *you*, as your full potential self, an evolutionary unique human joining with everyone everywhere** in evolutionary temples, mosques, synagogues, cathedrals, wherever evolutionary humans are emerging, yearning to give our greater gifts of love to the evolution of the world.

Remember these words:

> *Love God above all else,*
>
> *your neighbor as yourself,*
>
> *yourself as a natural Christ,*
>
> *a new human,*
>
> *an Evolutionary Unique Self.*

Combined with science and technology infused with love, you will all be changed. You are all being changed now. Let us be demonstrations of our own Conscious Evolution.

WHEN WE TALK ABOUT PRAYER, WHAT DO WE MEAN?

When we talk about prayer we want to actually evolve the word *church*, evolve the word *God*, and evolve what we mean when we talk about *prayer*. We want to step into the very source code of Reality itself and participate in this evolution.

So, when we talk about prayer, what do we mean?

Do we mean prayer to a Santa Claus god in the sky? No.

Do we mean prayer to a God who demands an abandonment of self and abandonment of goodness for the sake of obedience? No.

We told a story about a master earlier, who was making a blessing, and the blessing was *blessed are you. . .* and then, after that, there is a long text to the blessing that the pious would make every day before they ate or when they made grace after meals. But this master couldn't get past the third word. He'd go, *Blessed are you, you, you, you, you. Oh my god, YOU!*

That's prayer.

Prayer is the knowing that the personal face of the LoveIntelligence—that is the initiating and animating Eros of All-That-Is—*hears* our words.

Prayer is the knowing that the third face of God, God in the third person, is the evolutionary impulse that awakens throughout *all* of Reality. **The evolutionary impulse, which is the ceaseless creativity of Cosmos, that lives *in* Cosmos—and not merely *beyond* Cosmos—that pulses Reality, *that* evolutionary impulse, is the third face of God.**

The first face of God is when that evolutionary impulse, which is the LoveIntelligence of Reality, awakens *in* me, *as* me, and *through* me, when I realize that I am an Evolutionary Unique Self with gifts to give, a life to live, a poem to write, a song to sing that no one that ever was, is, or will be but myself can do.

The second face of God, God in the second person, is that infinite personal presence that knows my name. When I realize that every place I fall, I fall into God's hands—the *evolutionary* God, the LoveIntelligence that knows my name and affirms the dignity of my personal need.

When we pray, we ask for *everything*. We celebrate our finitude. We offer "Hallelujah," from Leonard Cohen. [*See appendix.*]

The song is the song by our great friend, Leonard Cohen, who sang about being able to be in life and realize that the complexity, the partial fulfillment, the cold floor, the disappointment, the heartache, and the joy, the beauty, the poignancy—it's all dignified because prayer affirms the dignity of our personal lives.

The words, *I've heard there was a secret chord that David played, and it pleased the Lord.* There's *a way in* through music, where I can hold—in the middle of the bafflement of life—*Hallelujah.*

> *It goes like this.*
> *The fourth, the fifth,*
> *the minor falls, the major lifts,*
> *the baffled King composing Hallelujah.*

Leonard Cohen does a verse about sexuality, the complexity of sexuality, and the pain of Eros.

It says:

> *Your faith was strong, but you needed proof.*
> *You saw her bathing on the roof.*

It's the story about David and Bathsheba, in the Bible, in the *Book of Kings.*

> *Her beauty in the moonlight overthrew you.*
> *She tied you to a kitchen chair.*
> *She broke your throne, and she cut your hair.*
> *From your lips, she drew the Hallelujah.*

In this meditation, we find a place in our life, whether in love and relationship and intimacy and sexuality or in life in general, where somehow, we felt *tied to the kitchen chair.* The throne broke. The hair was cut.

And yet, from that place, **we knew that although our hearts were broken, there's nothing more whole than a broken heart, and *from our lips, she drew the Hallelujah.***

Wow.

Feel the power of that.

Feel the power of this song.

Feel the power and the beauty.

> *You say I took the name in vain.*
> *I don't even know the name,*
>   *but if I did, really, what's it to you?*
> *There's a blaze of light in every word.*
> *It doesn't matter which you heard:*
>   *the holy or the broken Hallelujah.*

Friends, we are *all* holy *Hallelujahs*, and we are all broken *Hallelujahs*.

In the great mystery tradition, they say that in the Ark of the Covenant in Jerusalem where Solomon reigned (in the Indiana Jones movie, *Raiders of the Lost Ark,* is that Ark of the Covenant), the Mary Magdalene tradition comes from the tradition of the two cherubs in love above the ark, and the voice of God speaks *from between* the two cherubs.

In that tradition, the tablets that Moses, in the great biblical myth, is supposed to have received on Sinai—the first set of tablets were broken. Then, there was a second set of tablets that were whole. The mystical tradition teaches us that the whole tablets and the broken tablets *together* are in the Ark of the Covenant.

We're seeking our holy and our broken *Hallelujahs* because all pain, all rage, comes from not being able to live in the broken *Hallelujah*.

All politics of rage comes from *not* being able to build and live from the broken *Hallelujah*.

A politics of love is the response to a politics of rage.

A politics of love has fierce grace. It has anger at injustice, and it has the prophetic call to heal and transform reality—but it doesn't have rage out of control. It doesn't have bitterness. It doesn't have cynicism, so when we move from a politics of rage to a politics of love, we do it through a politics of empathy.

Empathy is the ability to know that all of us—you and me, all of us—live lives of partial fulfillment. **No one's fulfilled all the way, but the question is can I find the Outrageous Love, the joy, in *partial* fulfillment?** Can I turn my loneliness into loving?

It's from that place, my friends, that we pray.

We pray to the personal God that knows our name.

We pray to the personal God that is the evolutionary God.

We pray to the personal God that holds us every time we fall, and that is the LoveIntelligence, the evolutionary impulse pulsing in us, and in all of Reality.

Our prayer always is for *everything*. Prayer affirms the dignity of personal need, so when we pray, we ask for everything.

We pray for our health.

We pray for our strength.

We pray for our children, for our friends.

We pray for all of Reality.

We pray for evolution.

We pray for the evolutionary impulse.

We invite everyone to offer your prayers, so we can actually speak them into the noosphere, and let your prayer be a prayer for every person who's forgotten how to pray, for every person who thinks that prayer is just a fundamentalist idea to the obedient God who's ethnocentric and homophobic. No, that's not what prayer is.

Prayer is a movement, a turn towards the personal impulse of All-of-Reality that knows our name and holds us in every moment.

At this moment, the gates are open. The gates are open because we're here together.

I pray for all those who have forgotten how to pray, and for the part of *me* that may have forgotten how to pray, and for the part of me that doesn't remember that I'm always held in the arms of love. That's not a fundamentalist idea. That's not a regressive idea.

That's an *evolutionary* idea. That is the personal face of the evolutionary impulse, awake and alive.

JOINING GENIUS TO GIVE OUR GIFTS MORE FULLY INTO THE WORLD

An astonishing phrase from Jesus that I've always loved: *Ask and it is given.*

It doesn't say ask and it *will* be given. *Ask*, and it *is* given.

When you *ask* in the full recognition of it *being* so and get the feeling inside you of *the truth* of it being so, that what makes it so it is exactly *that*— because the so-ness of the ask of the prayer is *you*, one with the Divine, knowing it is so.

You are not really praying to an external being who then responds as much as *you're activating the inner impulse of yourself, that is the divine process of creation as you.*

Ask, and it is given.

How do we contribute to the politics of Evolutionary Love? We do it by creating a Field of Consciousness that awakens in each person—in each one of us, the impulse of evolution right in you, *feeling* the impulse—the divine love creating and expressing *your* unique genius and *your* special gift of love by joining genius with *others*.

In this field of intention and resonance, get in touch with that unique impulse of love in you, which is uniquely yours, that which you can do that nobody else on Earth can do, your special gift.

You are being guided by the mysterious force of evolution itself, to assist you in joining genius, with those you most need to give your gift, so when you give you become more of who you are— and so does the other.

The evolutionary politics of love is right there because giving our gift of love to one another is what activates it in ourselves. It's self-rewarding, and it serves the world in the same act.

Ask, and it is given.

Through this joining in the field, each of us is being born as what we like to call *a new human*, an evolutionary human, a Unique Evolutionary Self—in what we call *WeSpace*, "WE"-space of living creativity, each of us being born as a new human.

What do we mean by a new human? What's new about you or me?

Well, the world is new. Every second, every instant, it is emergent, so the new you is emerging, and with evolutionary eyes, you can feel and see and know that exact place where you are emerging.

In a WeSpace, where what's emerging in you is finding its connection with what's emerging in others, you're turning into the living love of life itself. As we confess our greatness to others, we are even more deeply inspired to find our vocation of destiny.

WHAT IS YOUR VOCATION OF DESTINY?

It's your unique gift to the shift:

- From fear to love
- From separation to convergence
- From winning *over* to joining *with*

We give so that each person, starting with yourself, can achieve more of what each of us really wants.

Just imagine creating more of what you most deeply want, need, and yearn for by joining genius with another, or others, who love your gift as much as you love theirs.

This is Evolutionary Love:

When you join genius with another, loving their gift as much as—or even more than—you love your own, what happens is that the two geniuses join and create newness, like genes, like sperm and egg.

Look at that, wow, creating a new miraculous person, an evolving person joining genius. To give our gift through joining genius is our heart's desire, in love with one another. **When we are in love with one another, joining genius, it creates more joy, more peace, more excitement *within* you, more awareness of God within you.**

What is the God within you if it is not the impulse of creation, creating *through* you?

- ◆ God creating,
- ◆ Creator creating,
- ◆ Co-creators creating, joining in love.

This is the vision of the politics of Evolutionary Love.

We are cultivating, together, the next stage of personal and social evolution.

In the past, we have had spiritual evolution on one hand—and *then* you move out into social, or scientific, or technological evolution. We are joined at the deepest spiritual impulse of our own vocation of destiny being given *through* joining with others.

Open the floodgates of the new society through you. Become a new person when you say *Yes* to the impulse of creativity.

- ◆ That *Yes*, right now, is opening the floodgates of love, of genius, of your unique greatness.

- That *Yes* fills you with the power to attract those you most need to give what you most yearn to give.

We are encouraging ourselves to give our gift of genius to each other— and to everyone who could possibly use it.

Imagine the outpouring of the gifts of love of the unique creativity of all:

- Feeling the impulse of the Divine in that giving
- Joining to evolve society through health, education, economic, science and technology, governments, environments as organs of your social body

That is the politics of Evolutionary Love.

We are going to go the whole way in this lifetime, to become whole beings to the next stage of human evolution.

Rather than joining our genes to have a miraculous child, we join genius to give our gifts more fully into the world.

RESPOND TO THE WORLD THAT IS UNLOVED

That is what we need at this moment of time: a politics of Evolutionary Love.

We set out a principle, a law of Evolutionary Love. We made a commitment.

We are forming together a new vision of Evolutionary Love and a politics of Evolutionary Love. In which every irreducible Unique Self—not just your Myers-Briggs test, but your irreducible Unique Self, your unique expression of the LoveIntelligence and LoveBeauty that is the animating Eros and energy of All-That-Is that lives *in* you, *as* you, and *through* you, that can be given only by you and you alone—responds to the world that remains *un-loved*, unless you stand on the abyss of that particular dimension of darkness and say, *Let there be light.*

61

We live in a world of outrageous pain and the only response to outrageous pain is Outrageous Love.

Outrageous Love means the *unique* expression of the LoveIntelligence that speaks through the *unique* configuration of light, which is your signature. We now know that every human being:

- Has a *unique* atomic signature
- Has a *unique* cellular signature
- Has a *unique* voice signature
- Has a *unique* light signature

That's the new realization that we've always known but we now have codified in the new texts of sacred science.

We know that: If any of us doesn't say, *let there be light*, there's going to be a darkness in the world that will never be lifted without each of us saying, *let there be light.*

If a particular person doesn't say, *let there be light* at the abyss of their particular unique need in their unique circle of intimacy and influence, then there will be darkness because that particular person has been asleep, a separate self. They haven't awakened as an Evolutionary Unique Self.

Let the light in me ignite the light in you.

We all live partially fulfilled lives but what do we do? We usually focus on the missing tile. There are a thousand tiles above us, and we look, we look, we look, and our eye catches the missing tile. We get caught in the missing-tile syndrome. The only thing we can see is the missing tile.

That's all we can see, instead of transforming that bitterness, that rage, that hurt into the joy of the celebration of every moment of finitude, the celebration of the infinite dignity of my personal life, the celebration of my story, which allows me to celebrate your story, which shatters jealousy, because I realized that all of *Reality intended my uniqueness,* and I'm living my story.

We get an Oscar for being the best possible us. If I try to be anyone else, we fail. We are the very best version that's possible.

That's the invitation to our lives, and *from that place*, we give our gifts, and we realize, oh my god, everyone's gifts are needed by All-That-Is because to be a Unique Self is the intention of Cosmos.

To be a Unique Self is to know that God intended you. Not the god you don't believe in but the God that is the intention of all of Reality.

God intended us. Each of us. God said billions of years ago, *Let me arrange the synchronicities of Reality so that we will incarnate, and at that particular moment of life give the unique gift that can be given only by us, that never was, is, or will be again.*

- ◆ Reality intended me.
- ◆ Reality adores me.
- ◆ The Universe feels love.
- ◆ Love's not hard to find.
- ◆ Love's impossible to avoid.
- ◆ That's not ordinary love.
- ◆ That's outrageous.
- ◆ It's Evolutionary Love.

It's the love that moves the sun and other stars. It's the love that is not mere human sentiment but the heart of existence itself. It's the love that drives us to create a global communion of pioneering souls. It's the love that drives each one of us to give our unique gift in our unique circle of intimacy and influence that can be given by us, and by us alone.

Let's just find each other in the utter delight of Evolutionary Love.

We chant from *the Inside of the Inside*. You can chant it to your partner, to your friend, to yourself, to anyone you're inviting to be part of your evolutionary family. Pick someone.

Get the words: our *holy and our broken Hallelujah,* because we wake up as the powerful expression of the evolutionary impulse not by bypassing outrageous pain, but by staring into outrageous pain with the knowing of our Outrageous Beauty, with the knowing that we are unique expressions of Evolutionary Love.

Chant to everyone you haven't talked to in ten years. It's time to pick up the phone; it's a part of us that we've cut off from, and anyone I'm living with every day, but I've forgotten to really tell them how much I love them, and the teller at the bank because love's not just romantic, sexual.

Love is "I see you."

Love is not just an emotion.

Love is a perception.

To be a lover, is to see with God's eyes.

Once we embrace *the holy and the broken Hallelujah,* we then need to go to the next step, and we need to confess our greatness, not to confess our weakness. We know about our broken *Hallelujah.* We've embraced that, but now, we need to realize that the essence of who you are is revealed in your moment of greatness.

PRACTICE CONFESSIONS OF GREATNESS

We hold each other's hands, and we look into each other's eyes, and we state this phrase:

> *By the authority vested in me by the great creating process, I see you. I'm seeing you with the eyes of the great creating process. Are you willing to speak to me as your own voice of the great creating process as you, so I can hear you speak it?*

Speak as the evolutionary impulse:

- I stand fearless in the face of fear.

- ◆ I stand fully certain in my power to change and transform in the face of uncertainty.
- ◆ I stand fully whole with my broken heart.
- ◆ I commit to playing a larger game.
- ◆ I commit to keep opening my heart.
- ◆ I commit to participate in the evolution of love.

After you've heard one person speak, you ask the other the same: *are you willing to speak in the voice of the great creating process within you, your highest expression of love?*

Dare to say, *my greatest impulse of expression and purpose is to participate in the planetary awakening in love through Unique Self Symphonies.*

Dare to speak the greatness that is uniquely your own, that word becomes flesh, that willingness to speak is imprinted in the noosphere or the thinking layer of Earth.

When the social layer comes alive through tweeting, through Facebook, through social media, something happens, but it doesn't necessarily happen positively. Wael Ghonin—who did the first Facebook post of a man who was killed by the Egyptian security force in Egypt years back, which actually launched through Facebook the great Arab Spring, the great uprising —wrote, *When I started, I thought that all we needed for the liberation of society was the internet.*

Then, what happened is that the fundamentalist horses came and essentially hijacked the internet, and the Arab Spring that the liberal community in America got so excited about essentially dissipated and got completely hijacked into more repression. Ghonin wrote two years later, *Now, I realize that for the liberation of society, we need the liberation of the internet itself.*

We are calling for:

- ◆ Can we invest the internet—the world of tweeting, the world of online platforms—with joy, respect, dignity, and a digital intimacy?

- Can we invest the internet with a digital intimacy in which we honor each other, and in which the internet becomes a source of joy and communion?
- Can we actually invest these sacred tools with a deep, profound *evolutionary* commitment, and create the Unique Self Symphony of pioneering souls playing on the internet that actually changes and shifts it all?

To know that when we speak our highest with each other, we are the great creating process. It's a very intimate, wonderful form of communion.

The noosphere, *the thinking layer of Earth* as Teilhard de Chardin called it, is through each one of us speaking our word in communion at this level of intensity. Our joining of love is affecting the thinking layer. It is not only just one-on-one who's speaking, because the nervous system of the planetary body is alive with the voices of the members of the planetary body.

We're adding our divine voices of love into the noosphere—consciously.

We invite as many human beings as possible to place their gift of love into that pantheon, the nervous system of the planet. **Every word we're saying is global, as well as local.**

We affirm in the confessions of greatness through the great communions of pioneering souls joining genius, through the authority of life itself, to speak our voices into the Unique Self Symphony. When we can do it live and loud, we're going to actually do it.

We confess delight and commitment to make the world better and to give unique gifts into the noosphere, convening together with all of our friends, all of the leaders around the world who are participating, a **Planetary Awakening in Love through Unique Self Symphonies in which the politics of Evolutionary Love becomes a politics of empathy, a politics of evolutionary intimacy.**

The new politics of Evolutionary Love is giving an evolutionary party to those who seek to express their creativity, by joining genius with others to create the evolutionary party, to celebrate evolving humans joining, to give our gift to the evolution of ourselves and our world.

We are an evolutionary party. Oh my god. The evolutionary party replaces the tea party. *Amen. Amen. Amen.*

What an utter and complete and total delight it is to be alive in this moment.

We're learning together as we go. We're learning, learning, learning, learning, but the most important thing is we're laying down the tracks of what might be a new institution into Reality that we're going to create together, which is the evolution of love.

CHAPTER FIVE

REALITY IS INTELLIGENT AND ALIVE, ENCODED WITH A DIRECTION TOWARDS HIGHER ORDERS OF OUTRAGEOUS LOVE

Episode 5 — December 3, 2016

WE ARE EVOLUTIONARY LOVERS!

It's so deeply good to be awake and alive.

We are going to be laying down the tracks of a personal politics of Evolutionary Love. We're going to move from a politics of rage, to a politics of love, and from a politics of fear, to a politics of empathy.

We are always going to be not politically correct but spiritually *incorrect*. Let us be spiritually incorrect together. Let us rock it open. Let us love it open.

In Reality, there are always two choices: to be open, or to be closed.

We're excited. People say, *what are you so excited about, you evangelicals?*

Yes, we're evolutionary evangelicals. Evangelism means there's *good* news.

The Universe is a love story. *The Universe: A Love Story* is going somewhere. We are part of where it is going. We are personally implicated in the evolutionary process.

We get excited about it. We are Evolutionary Lovers! We are evolutionary evangelicals, awake and alive together.

This week, we want to recapitulate this new vision of this politics of love.

Our purpose is not wisdom-tainment, like spiritual entertainment.

- We are laying down tracks.
- We are participating in the evolution of love.
- We are coming together in this global communion of pioneering souls.
- We are evolving the source code.
- We are going to change the game.

Let's go higher. Let's do it together. Let's love it open.

EVOLUTIONARY CHAKRA MEDITATION

Breathe in, deeply, the whole story of creation.

Place your attention now on Source, on the source of evolution, on the mind of God.

Breathe in from that source, all that was, is now, and will be, from the first two seconds of the Big Bang.

See now the evolutionary spiral unfolding—energy, matter, life, the biosphere, single-celled life, animal life, human life.

And now we, humans, are going around the next turn on the spiral of evolution, facing the destruction of all life on Earth or the evolution of life to its next stage.

Breathe in this multi-billion-year story of creation into your lowest chakra. **Feel the security coming through your body, of that core of the spiral of evolution, carrying the genius of all that came before us, into the lowest chakra of your body, and feel secure.**

Now returning once again to the mind of God.

Feel the power of that process of creation entering your regenerative organs. And place that huge impulse of creativity, and see yourself shifting from degeneration toward regeneration, from massive procreation toward co-creation.

Feel the awakening of the immense power of the generative organs through the impulse of evolution.

Now breathe up once again through the mind of God:

- Through the billions of years of evolution
- Through your impulse of security
- Through your tremendous powers of regeneration and co-creation

Place that power into your security of your mid-power center.

- The power of your presence
- The power of your greatness
- The power of your uniqueness

Breathe the entire impulse into that power center and send it out into the world.

Consciously expressing the power of that impulse as you in the world. With all your genius coded in it. Radiate that creativity and power.

Starting once again in the mind of God, in one deep breath, bring that impulse of evolution into your heart. Carrying the frequency and genius of the whole process into your heart of unconditional love.

Love of the entire story of creation.

Love of all that came before you.

Love of everyone on Earth.

Starting with those you most love—your sister, your brother, your mother, your father, your child, your friend, your community of influence.

Now, let that impulse of love just go further. Let it reach out into the global communion of pioneering souls—everywhere on Earth. Just like us. Awakening to their own inner impulse of creativity. And your touch of love is now touching them in the vast domain of universal intelligence.

Now, bring that impulse of evolution further up into the heart and feel it as your gift of love, your vocation, your calling, your intention to create. Place that mighty core of the spiral of evolution into your vocation, in your upper heart.

Feel your gift of love going out, uniquely you, expressing that which you are given to give, with the joy in the giving of it, to all you love and beyond.

Now, going once again up from the mind of God, through all the chakras of your being, breathe the impulse into your throat. **Let your voice vibrate when you speak with the resonance of creation, the frequency of vibration of the impulse as you.** Sound your note with this impulse of power and creativity.

Now bring the impulse of evolution all the way up from Source, energy, matter, life, animal life, through your own security, generative organs, power, vocation of heart. Bring it up through your throat into your third eye. Activate the supramental genius of the whole process of creation embodied in you. It's true.

At the precise moment, contact your expression of the divine process, as you, at the threshold of your own evolution.

At the precise moment, when the evolution of the world is shifting from one stage to the next.

71

Place the genius and power of your impulse of creation into the scales of history, towards more life, more love, more genius, in the great 13.8-billion-year tradition of evolution.

We could say *Hallelujah* evolution!

Breathe the impulse all the way up and all the way down.

You, and we, are the whole story of creation, coming to you in person.

THE ESSENTIAL PRACTICE OF RECLAIMING PRAYER

We realize that *the god you don't believe in, doesn't exist.* Meaning, the old image of god as the one demanding obedience, standing there ready to punish you if you just missed a fraction of a fraction, is not actually the deepest understanding we have.

The deepest understanding we have based on the best of the interior sciences of all the great traditions, based on the best of evolutionary science, and chaos theory, and complexity theory, is that Reality is intelligent, Reality is alive.

Prayer is the realization that Reality is intelligent and alive. Reality manifested photosynthesis, mitosis and meiosis, and the cortex and neocortex before there were supercomputers.

Mitosis and meiosis are more dazzlingly complex and beautiful than anything we've been able to manifest with every supercomputer that ever existed.

Meaning, Reality is awake. Reality is alive.

Remember *The Sound of Music: The hills are alive?*

Reality is alive.

Reality is intelligent.

Reality is awake.

Reality is breathing.

Prayer means something really simple:

> *I speak, and an intelligent Reality—the LoveBeauty*
> *and LoveIntelligence of Reality—hears me.*
> *The noosphere—the awake, alive, intelligent Reality—*
> *hears my voice.*

We used to talk about God as the Infinity of Power. Not God *out there*. But God that holds it all, and God that's in it all. The inherent ceaseless creativity of Cosmos, that at the same time *is* the source of Cosmos, and all power participates in that power.

And yet, that's an insufficient way to speak of essence in the Divine.

God is not only the Infinity of Power, God is the Infinity of Intimacy.

Intimacy means that every part of our life is beautiful, even when it's tragic; that we sometimes live in partial fulfillment; that we are all *holy and broken Hallelujahs.*

We realize that *Hallelujah*, the great psalm of King David, sung by Leonard Cohen, is always our first prayer song. We realize, every breath is *Hallelujah*, the celebration of finitude.

Prayer affirms the dignity of personal need.

Prayer affirms the infinite dignity of our intimate lives in all their dimensions. "Hallelujah," by Leonard Cohen. [*See appendix.*]

> *There's a blaze of light in every word, it doesn't matter which you heard.*
> *The holy or the broken Hallelujah.*
> *I did my best but it wasn't much.*
> *I couldn't feel, so I tried to touch.*
> *I've told the truth, I didn't come to fool you.*

And even though it all went wrong,

I'll stand before the Lord of song,

with nothing on my lips, but Hallelujah.

And *Hallelujah* is: *Yah.* It's the second part of the word Hallelu-yah. It's the outbreath. It's the *Pranayama* of Reality itself (Pranayama being a word drawn from the Eastern traditions). And *hallel*, pristine praise, delight. And *holelut—hallel*, the same root word in Hebrew, means drunken stupor. It's the *holy and the broken Hallelujah.* It's prayer which affirms the dignity of personal need.

If God is only the Infinity of Power—a mistake in the evolution of consciousness—we need to evolve our understanding, our realization of the Divine. If God is only the Infinity of Power, then it's but us who are relatively powerless to be obedient. But **if God is also the Infinity of Intimacy, then not only do we need to claim our power, but we need to claim the infinite adequacy and dignity of our lives.**

The personal matters. No one is extra on the set. We can't do it without each other.

And all of a sudden, we understand that there's a problem of evil. Evil is a failure of intimacy. We have to respond to evil, to suffering, by restoring intimacy.

Every single person is intended by Reality to be a Unique Self. The implication of uniqueness is to know that Reality intended me.

Feel into that…

When you actually *feel* that, you can actually have—we call it in the East, a *kensho*—an immediate enlightenment experience.

Oh my god, *Reality intended me, Reality needs me!*

So when I pray, I pray to the intelligent Cosmos that knows my name,

that intended me, that holds me.

The Infinity of Intimacy, which is all of the cosmic infinite laws of physics, laws of chemistry, billions of light years, sitting in a chair right in front of me, looking at me, saying:

I need you, I love you, I care for you. You matter so infinitely to me.

Do not forget *personal* prayer. Do not just pray *generally.*

You matter.

Your life matters.

Your loneliness matters.

Don't get caught in life as a victim.

Don't get caught in the pathos of a story that you can't get out of.

Affirm the dignity of your story.

Your story matters infinitely.

Feel the power of prayer. The power of prayer, not as a fundamentalist prayer, not as a fundamentalist God who says: *Worship me, and if you don't, you're damned forever, and only my people are safe.*

But actually, **the realization that that which unites us is so much greater than that which divides us.** And that the LoveIntelligence of Reality is holding us in every second. And that every moment of our lives, from our lips is drawn the *Hallelujah*: the drunken stupor, the pristine praise, the inbreath and the outbreath.

No one is extra on the set.

Our prayers matter. We become prayer. We are prayer.

As Evolutionary Evangelicals and activists, we are for the transformation of it all.

WE ARE HERE TO GENTLE THE BIRTH TO THE NEXT STAGE OF EVOLUTION

We have entered the first age of Conscious Evolution.

Now this is an amazing thought: Evolution has been going on for billions and billions of years but no species *knew* they were part of it.

There were five mass extinctions before we got here. Billions of species have been extinct.

None of them *knew* it was happening.

And here we are now, this young human species. As far as species go, we are very young.

We are just waking up with the realization that we are the power of evolution.

We've been given the power to destroy ourselves through all our advanced technologies and capabilities. And, at the very same instant of awakening, **we are aware that we could evolve ourselves towards a future that is radically new**. As once human life was new.

So just place ourselves in this message at that actual shift point, 13.8 billion years of evolution, to right this moment. **The first species on Earth ever to be aware of evolution, aware we're creating ourselves by every thought, everything we do, every baby we have, every war we fight.**

We gather together the pioneering souls of Earth to move evolution by choice, not chance.

Conscious Evolution: evolution by choice, not chance.

To choose more life, more love, more freedom, in the 13.8-billion-year tradition.

From the mind of God, for billions of years, every time there has been a turn of the spiral—from single-celled life, to multi-celled life, to animal life, to human life—every single turn, there is a new sense of direction, towards greater complexity (as from single-celled to multi-celled to animal), leading to greater freedom and intelligence.

That's why we have all these cells joining together in ever more complex bodies. Like our 52 trillion cells talking to 52 trillion cells each, each cell uniquely creating us, organized way beyond what any human could possibly do. We are right at this stage of more freedom, more creativity.

Feel into it. . .

Feel right now, the desire to *be* more, to *love* more, to *create* more, to be *more connected*, following internally the impulse of evolution, which leads from complexity, to freedom, to more synergistic or loving order.

The Universe: A Love Story.

And the great evolutionary teacher, Teilhard de Chardin, had the assumption that the next stage of evolution is when the noosphere, he called it, *the thinking layer*—now the internet, the social media—gets its collective eyes. If it's infused with enough love, creativity, in the tradition of evolution itself, he believed it would turn on, and he called it, as a Jesuit, *the Christ-ification of the Earth.*

We're calling it *the awakening of the planet in love through a Unique Self Symphony.* In other words, we have the expectation of the possibility of humanity connecting in love.

Following the great impulse of all of evolution, what seems to be the intention of the Creator of evolution? **It appears to us that the intention of the Creator, of the billions of years of evolution, is to create co-creators.**

Doesn't that seem right?

That the intention of God is to create godlings.

The intention of the entire process—toward higher freedom, greater consciousness, and more loving order—is to create beings able to say *Yes* to the intention of creation itself. Not simply as an idealistic thing but simply as saying *Yes* to the entire process of creation.

We are in an *evolving* universe.

It's not in any religion.

It's not coded in any politics.

It's not known broadly, even in our universities.

Even Einstein thought it was an *eternal* universe. It is an eternal and evolving universe.

Here's how it happened.

In the 1960s, two radio astronomers picked up the background radiation of the first "flaring-forth," as Brian Swimme called it, or the First Big Bang. They were able to record this vibrational field from the origin of creation. They were able to understand that in those first two seconds, as they say, the attunement was so perfect, the energy was so perfectly designed, that it made it possible for energy, matter, life, and us to happen.

If the frequencies in that first two seconds had been a little faster or a little slower—the scientists have told us—we wouldn't exist at all. And to the degree that the scientists think it's an accidental universe, to that degree, they cannot explain the perfection of the first two seconds.

It is not only the perfection of the first two seconds, but that **the universe is coded with *direction*.**

That humanity is becoming more loving, more creative, more empathetic, naturally, we're pointing to the study of the 13.8 billion years of direction in evolution. This is not a made-up story; this is coded in our blood and bones.

We're cultivating the genius of evolution.

When we say genius, we don't mean you're just brighter than somebody else. We mean, the awesome, supramental creativity of organizing an entire universe, including you, being the impulse of evolution, that's *in* you, now yearning to be more, love more, do more, and create more, at the instant of Conscious Evolution on this Earth.

Is that a moment?

Is that a moment to celebrate?

If we didn't have some place to go to recognize the incredible intelligence and love and to find ourselves the first generation in the history of these billions of years, as far as we know, on planet Earth, to be alive to saying *Yes* to it, by free choice.

When we say *Yes* to this impulse, we are actually saying *Yes* to the mind of God.

We're not doing this alone. You see, sometimes you might feel you're inadequate. You might sometimes not feel you would know enough to help evolve our species. Isn't that true?

Realize you *are* the evolution of the species incarnate. **Every single breath you're taking that's longing, desiring, and yearning for more, *is* the God-Force internalized.**

This is not about expecting the second coming of Christ in that old language, but we *are* expecting a planetary awakening in love.

- We are expecting that the direction of evolution leads toward higher consciousness, greater freedom, more complex order.
- We are expecting that if we create a convergence zone—a vehicle of inspiration for all of us, anywhere on Earth, who choose to give this gift of love, empathy, creativity, and genius, to evolve ourselves and our society—that the self-organizing Universe will do the rest.

Again, we couldn't have invented photosynthesis, we couldn't have invented our bodies.

We are here to gentle the birth to the next stage of evolution. To gather the empathy, creativity, in the politics of love.

What are the elements of that, such that we actually will wake it up in our lifetime before we go down towards greater destruction?

Let us gentle the birth to the next stage of conscious self-evolution.

YOUR LOVE STORY IS A CHAPTER IN THE LOVE STORY OF REALITY ITSELF

The great flaring forth of Reality is the unrelenting affirmation of the dignity, the positivity, of Reality.

The great Big Bang is a holy *Yes!*

We know in quantum physics today, and we know in the interior sciences of enlightenment, that the universe actually flashes in and out of existence. It's the nature of virtual reality; what we call virtual existence.

In every moment, Reality is being renewed, both from the perspective of physics and from the perspective of interior science.

Why is that so? Because actually, in every second, Reality is crying out: *Yes, Yes, Yes!*

What's the most essential truth?

This emerges not *against* science. This is the deepest implication of the leading edges of the *evolutionary* sciences and the best and deepest understanding of all the great traditions of wisdom in the premodern, modern, and postmodern periods. As we head into this new expression, this new moment in history, we are articulating the memory of the future.

Sometimes, to heal you need to recover a memory of the past, and that's critical in trauma. But sometimes, **to heal and transform you need to recover a memory of the future.**

We are here to articulate the memory of the future.

Hope is a memory of the future.

Life is not as Shakespeare' Macbeth said it was: *a tale told by an idiot, full of sound and fury signifying nothing.* It's not *tomorrow, and tomorrow, and tomorrow, that creeps in this petty pace, day after day to the last syllable of recorded time.*

No! It's *tomorrow*, and tomorrow, and tomorrow! And *Yes!*

The Universe, Reality, is not a fact. Reality is a story; that's the best understanding of science we have today.

It's *going somewhere.* Reality has *telos*, it means direction. Reality has Eros, aliveness.

We live in a *telerotic universe.*

Reality is not a fact, it's a story.

But it's not an ordinary story—it's *a love story.*

But it's not an ordinary love story—**it's an Outrageous Love Story.**

That is the best understanding of Reality that we have today, based on the best integration of all the sciences from all the different disciplines.

Let's recapitulate the distinctions:

- We distinguished between ordinary love and Outrageous Love.
- Ordinary love is a strategy of the ego, seeking comfort and security, and we dress it up in the pretty costume of love.
- Outrageous Love is something else. Outrageous Love is Evolutionary Love.

- ◆ Outrageous Love is the love that moves the sun and other stars, said Dante.
- ◆ Outrageous Love, said Tagore, the Bengali mystic, Outrageous Love is *not mere human sentiment, it's the heart of existence itself.*

So what does that mean for me?

Reality is not a fact, it's a story.

But it's not an ordinary story, it's *a love story.*

But it's not an ordinary love story, it's an Outrageous Love Story.

It means that I have to awaken to who I really am, to know my true nature. The only sanity is to be madly in love. **To be madly in love is the only sane way to live.**

Why? Because that is the nature of Reality. Every quark falls in love with another quark. Attraction, electromagnetic attraction, allurement is the core of Reality. All the way up and all the way down the evolutionary chain is allurement, attraction, and love.

Reality moves towards greater and greater levels of mutuality, recognition, union and embrace. And that's *Hallelujah.* Not because it is a dogma; it is a *dharma.* This is what we call *First Principles and First Values.*[1]

Dharma means the best take we have on Reality today.

The only way to be sane is to be madly in love. And not to be madly in love with just one person; don't exile love to romantic sexual love. Romantic

---

1 First Principles and First Values are a weaving together of the most crucial, validated truths from all the wisdom streams—premodern, modern, and postmodern—into a new whole greater than the sum of its parts. First Principles woven together with First Values are the plotlines of what we have called the Story of Value that is the inherent motivational and erotic architecture of Reality. First Principles and First Values are urgently needed—personally and collectively—to respond to the catastrophic and even existential risks that challenge us, invite us, and demand our response at this moment in time. First Principles and First Values are ancient, time-honored, and venerable, even as they are evolutionary, emergent, and new. See David J. Temple, *First Principles and First Values* (2024).

sexual love is gorgeous, it's beautiful. But to exile love to that narrow band of love, is to misunderstand and to make love small.

Outrageous Love means we get to be outrageously in love with each other, as quarks are outrageously in love with each other, and we uniquely get to see and rejoice in each other, because we awaken as Outrageous Love. We are Outrageous Lovers.

What do Outrageous Lovers do?

Outrageous Lovers keep every boundary that should be kept, and they break every boundary that should be broken.

Which boundaries should be broken?

- The boundaries of contraction.
- The boundaries of smallness.
- The boundaries of limiting beliefs.
- The boundaries of I'm an extra on the set.

An Outrageous Lover commits Outrageous Acts of Love.

Which Outrageous Acts of Love does an Outrageous Lover commit?

Those that are a function of your Unique Self.

What's a Unique Self?

A Unique Self is not a Myers-Briggs test. It's not a typology. It's not just my talent. My Unique Self is the best answer, based on the best sciences, interior and exterior, to the three greatest questions that will ever be asked in our lives.

The questions are:

- Who are you?
- Why are you here?
- What's there to do?

You are an irreducibly unique expression of the LoveIntelligence and LoveBeauty that is the initiating and animating energy of All-That-Is, that lives in you, as you, and through you, that never was, is, or will be ever again, other than through you.

And as such, you have an irreducibly unique perspective. You are a unique taste, a unique quality of intimacy. That unique perspective and unique quality of intimacy manifests your unique capacity to give your unique gift, to offer your unique vision, which addresses a unique need, in your unique circle of intimacy and influence, that could be addressed only by you.

Which means that you are called, I am called, to stand on the abyss of darkness. And with your unique singularity, your unique structure of light, to actually say: Let there be light!

That you speak to a corner of the world that is unloved. That no one that ever was, is, or will be, other than you, can speak to.

Reality is somehow deficient without you waking up and saying, *I'm here to give my unique gift.*

Werner Erhard created the Landmark Forum, which is so beautiful but is actually limited at a certain point. From Werner's perspective, ultimately, it's all empty and meaningless. And *even the fact that it's empty and meaningless,* he says, *is empty and meaningless. So go create your Reality.*

Now that's true, other than one little thing…

What's true is: you can create the Reality.

What's true is: you can transform.

But what's not true is: it's empty and meaningless.

It's infinitely meaningful. All of it is meaningful.

What's empty and meaningless are the old patterns, the contractions.

But actually, Reality waits for you.

It's not just that you create whatever you want. Actually, you're *needed*.

Your irreducibly unique molecular signature, and your subatomic signature, and your cellular signature, was intended and designed by Reality.

You are a unique gorgeous expression of Reality and LoveIntelligence that is desperately desired and needed and affirmed by All-That-Is.

So wow!

Reality is having a *you* experience.

And here's the story. If Reality is having that experience and we need another person, we can be madly in love with that person. We can be so excited that others are doing what they can do because we don't have their capacities. So there's no need for jealousy between us; we get to love each other madly. We say, *oh my god, we are in devotion. We are in adoration.*

We are here.

We are committed.

We are committed to offering a vision of transformation, which is rooted in the best of science and the best of spirit, which is the good news, which is the best understanding we have today.

Reality is a love story. Your love story, the love story of your life, is a chapter in the love story of Reality itself.

We used to confess our sins, now we confess our greatness:

I am a beautiful being capable of loving.

I am a beautiful being with this particular gift to give, whatever your greatness is.

I am a beautiful being with this message that can be given.

I'm a wild Outrageous Lover.

I'm going to keep making mistakes in the right direction.

I'm committed to Evolutionary Love.

Confess our greatness.

I am love itself.

I'm an amazingly vibrant and living being.

Confess the gift that's yours to give.

CHAPTER SIX

LONELINESS AS AN EVOLUTIONARY DRIVER

Episode 6 — December 10, 2016

WHAT IS THE RESPONSE TO OUR ALONENESS?

We are not alone. We are coming home. Those of us in whom the flame of expectation burns are an emerging evolutionary family upon Earth. We have been scattered everywhere, in order to seed the global culture with the awareness and love of life ever evolving. We are each an expression of the Divine process of creation.

We are here to birth a species:

- Capable of loving one another as ourselves
- Capable of overcoming the illusion of separate self
- Able to be one with the whole, a puzzle piece within the whole puzzle
- Awakening to the impulse of evolution as an expression of our own Unique Selves evolving

We are a resonant field—for the evolving humans—as a **home base** for the appearance and nurturing of co-creators of the emerging world.

Do we feel loneliness?

Yes, we do.

What is the response to our aloneness? Interiority, genuine holy conversation, and purpose.

As we join together as members of the evolutionary family of humanity, we begin to foster the politics of Evolutionary Love. Consciously.

We're finding our way home. Reality flows through our blood and bones, as the impulse of the Creator, animating us as unique evolutionary co-creators.

EMERGENT WORLD VISION: THE UNIVERSE IS A LOVE STORY

Oh, my god!

Are we excited? We are excited. Now, why are we excited? Are you allowed to get excited? If you're excited, you must be an evangelist.

We are evangelists, yes!

We are not evangelists of fundamentalism.

We are evangelists who are bringing the good news together.

We are all bringing the good news. And the good news is that there's a vision.

The good news is that we stand at the abyss of uncertainty—and there's an emergent world vision.

We know a lot.

We know that the Universe is a love story:

- It's a love story that we are *personally* implicated in.
- We can actually *awaken as Outrageous Love* in that love story.

- We are about awakening to the evolutionary impulse that lives in us, as us, and through us.
- The evolutionary impulse each of us has an irreducibly unique expression of that LoveIntelligence and LoveBeauty—and as such, has unique Outrageous Acts of Love to commit that can be done by you and by you alone.

So we are excited. We are evangelists. We are bringing the good news.

We are in chapter seven:

Seven is completion.

Seven is wholeness.

Seven is Sabbath.

Seven, in Hebrew, is *sheva*: utter satisfaction, as something begins to be grounded in Reality.

WHAT FUNDAMENTALISTS GOT RIGHT

We deepen the field of evolutionary prayer. We reclaim prayer in a deep way. Each time there is new wine in old flasks.

What does loneliness have to do with our meta-vision, which is to articulate a personal politics of Evolutionary Love?

The fundamentalists got something right that the liberal left-wing world completely missed. You know what they got right? *The Lord Jesus knows your name and speaks to you directly, and you can speak to Jesus, and Jesus is holding you.* Okay, you got that, that's a little fundamentalism.

Now, the truth is, we might not like the way they do it. There's a lot of things we don't like about fundamentalism; it's xenophobic, and it's a little homophobic, and it's politically way far to the right, and it's against free choice and abortion. We have all the problems.

But what did they get right?

They got something really right. What they got right is, *Jesus knows your name.*

When I say Jesus, I don't mean Jesus. I don't mean a particular Christian expression. I mean the personal face of Reality, we call it *the second face of God.*

Friends, we are on *the Inside of the Inside.*

THE THREE FACES OF GOD

The first face of God is *I Am*, in Buddhism. You go to an ashram, I Am. *Tat tvam asi*: Thou art That. The divine impulse that lives in me, as me, and through me; the evolutionary impulse awakening in me. In the Eastern world, *tat tvam asi*, it's the divine principle in me. It's what they call in Buddhism, *sunyata*, or emptiness. It is *Shiva Shakti* that lives as me. In evolutionary spirituality, it's the evolutionary impulse awakening *as me*. That's the first face of God.

The third face of God is the forces of physics, the incessant creativity of Cosmos, the Evolutionary Love that drives all of Reality. That's third person, third face of God.

But we've missed the second face of God, which is the personal face of the evolutionary impulse that knows your name, that holds you, that holds you no less than when you're held in a conversation with another. The realization that I live in an Intimate Universe, and that every place I fall, I fall into God's hands. That I can stand and pray, and for as long as I stand and pray, God is going to stand and listen.

- God is not *less* than the personal; God is the infinity of the personal.
- God is not *less* than human intimacy; God is the Infinity of Intimacy that knows my name.

90

- ◆ The god you don't believe in doesn't exist.

Divinity is always a trinity, the Catholics got that right.

- ◆ The Eastern Buddhist world just gets the first face of God but leaves out the second face.
- ◆ Christians often only get the second face, and leaves out the first face, leaves out that *I Am God*, leaves out *tat tvam asi*: Thou Art That, leaves out the evolutionary impulse awaking in me.
- ◆ Science—our colleague, Stuart Kauffman, for example, at the Santa Fe Institute—gets the third face of God: the incessant ceaseless creativity, or the evolutionary impulse.
- ◆ In evolutionary spirituality, we forget the second face of God: God knows my name. God is holding me intimately.

The fundamentalist world is actually holding this sense of the second face of God, but they've hijacked that into a fundamentalist world which says: *that second face of God is owned by me.* It's owned by Islam. It's owned by Christianity. It's owned by Judaism. *We own it, and we know exactly what God says. And God happens to have fundamentalist politics. And God happens to be an extreme right winger.*

Well, that's not true.

That's a hijacking of the second face of God.

But if we just reject the second face of God, we are living in denial. We are living in denial of the Intimate Universe.

We have a historic mission. **We are reclaiming the second face of God that knows our name and hears us, before whom we say** *Hallelujah.*

Let's hear another evolutionary personality, Leonard Cohen, who was both a Buddhist and a Jew, and he's doing Sabbath, and he's doing Christianity, and he's singing the Psalms of David. He's singing *Hallelujah.*

91

THE FIELD OF EVOLUTIONARY PRAYER

We hold silence of presence, which is the aftertaste of a chant or a prayer.

It's in the aftertaste; it's in the silence of presence that we live. And in that silence of presence, we affirm, as Cohen does in "Hallelujah," the dignity of our loneliness, the dignity of the holy and the broken *Hallelujah*.

> *She tied you to a kitchen chair.*
> *She broke your throne.*
> *She cut your hair.*
> *And from your lips, she drew the Hallelujah.*

And *she* here is not a woman or man. She is life. She is *the broken and the holy Hallelujah*.

Prayer affirms the dignity of our yearning.

Prayer affirms the dignity of personal need.

Prayer affirms the dignity of our loneliness.

When we offer prayer, we pray from the dignity of that loneliness, from the dignity of that personal need. We break out, and we pray for ourselves and we pray for another. **We pray and we ask for *everything*.** Not just for world peace, though. We ask for our uncle Sam, who needs help. Or my brother Jack, who's having an operation next week, and for my own ability to support my family.

We actually know that, in this moment, the gates are open.

We actually offer our prayers.

We offer *Hallelujah*.

And in Hebrew *Hallelujah* is drunken intoxication, and *Hallelujah* is praise.

We pray for *everything*.

We pray because in prayer we affirm the dignity of personal need.

We are not afraid to pray. Every place we're on our knees, we're on our knees to God. **We open the gates, and we invite everyone, and we invite ourselves, to be an unguarded heart and *learn* prayer, so we can actually pray together.** And we say *amen* to every prayer.

When we open our hearts to pray, when we actually speak the prayer out loud, *something happens.*

OVERCOMING LONELINESS BY SAYING "YES" TO THE IMPULSE OF EVOLUTION WITHIN US

The first step beyond loneliness is to know that although sometimes we may live lives of quiet desperation, we are never alone.

We reclaim the *Infinity of Intimacy.*

We get connected to that *Infinity of Intimacy.*

We step out of our loneliness.

We are always held in the arms of the Infinity of Intimacy, that intended us, that desires us, that knows our name.

The Infinity within us is always there and is so easy to lose.

Loneliness is possibly the most prevalent emotional problem we face in this culture. More people feel lonely than any other psychological problem. It's obvious what happened. The extended family disappeared. Most of us do not live in a community. There are minimal services to help us. Depression can sink in.

Use loneliness to realize something more wants to be expressed. Vocation— life purpose—a great key to overcoming loneliness. Follow the impulse of evolution. Create a new family and keep it growing and growing. Find your evolutionary family of humanity who now has said *Yes* to a deeper purpose.

And saying *Yes* can sometimes *separate* us from daily life, the family that we grew up with, the husbands or wives we may have had, even the children. You will find yourself breaking very, very comfortable patterns.

The impulse of doing more, being more, loving more, true life purpose in each one of us, seeking evolutionary family and challenging each other to move further onward, can be trusted and we often need to step beyond what we might feel is very secure.

We all leave places that are secure in our lives.

What is the forgotten hope?

To emerge structures that create the strength and the home for the politics of Evolutionary Love to be nurtured in the human family that will not go away—a most important step in this vast movement of political evolutionary change.

Here's a quote from Ilia Delio, a great Catholic nun, and a student of Teilhard de Chardin:

> You cannot remain Catholic, unless you understand the new cosmology. The less you understand that the universe is filled with the impulse of the Divine, and that Divine is in you, and there is no three-tiered universe: God above, hell below, this is wrong. You cannot expect to remain a Catholic and believe the three-tier universe, it's wrong.

The Universe is a love story.

It started at the origin of creation with an impulse to connect, connect, connect: quarks with electrons, with protons, with neutrons, with people, given this enormous inspiration to reach out with life purpose, to connect and to love others in a politics of love.

We are a Planetary Awakening in Love through Unique Self Symphonies. Our overall goal is to reach out and to invite people everywhere in the world who are moving towards being co-creators, to join together their creativity and their love until we can infuse the noosphere, the thinking layer of Earth, with our love.

This is what the Catholics said was *the second coming of Christ*. **What we and the planetary mission are working toward is the evolutionary awakening of love on a mass scale.**

Use loneliness as an evolutionary driver. Express love. Have holy conversations.

The first thing to know is that we are *one* with the impulse of evolution, our *interiority*. Get in touch with that interior Reality. Perhaps, it's a process of morning meditation; quieting the mind, then writing in your journal the situations you're facing, like *I'm lonely*, or the worst situations you can possibly think of.

And then say, *dearly Beloved, what does this mean?* And turn off my thinking mind, and tune into the deeper knowing of Reality. Discover it's totally *inside*. Tap into the interiority. Read it, be guided by it, and learn from it. And then the next day, say, *here's what happened, dearly Beloved. It didn't work*, or *this is great*. **Have very profound conversations with the dearly Beloved interiority.**

OVERCOMING LONELINESS WITH PURPOSE

We have to identify the actions we are taking toward a politics of love that only you can do *uniquely*.

+ Purpose is not just: *I have a nice project.*
+ Purpose is not even just so I can go get a good job doing X, Y, or Z.
+ Purpose is tuning in through the interiority, with the impulse of that divine creativity within you, and saying *Yes* to it.

Does that feel right to say *Yes* to the inner impulse? It is Unique Self expressing.

Saying yes activates the divine presence of creative force within you.

The holy *Yes* that set the Big Bang. Holy *Yes*. Say *Yes* to your life— the biggest, deepest, greatest thing you are saying *Yes* to.

And let's say *Yes* together.

What does this *Yes* do? It brings us closer to union with the Divine. We become non-dual. Because if the *Yes* is deep enough, as it is in so many of us—it means that we and the impulse have become *one*. You and the impulse, when your *Yes* is profound, you and the inner impulse become one. As Jesus said: *If you've seen me, if you've seen yourself, you've seen the Divine Creator.*

And the deeper meaning of the word co-creator is *one with the Creator within*. If we have any understanding of God's intention, the Creator, it's to create co-creators.

And how do we get to be one with God? By saying *Yes* to our unique creativity.

The holy *Yes*, in the holy interiority, with the holy conversations that we are going to have, so we can remind ourselves and realize we are not alone in our *Yes*. Because if you're saying *Yes* all by yourself, it's extremely lonely, even if you're very, very great, so we consciously create what we call a *WeSpace*: a resonant field of two or more who are truly excited by what you want to give.

It's very important that they are excited by you, and you can be equally excited by them. But it's not okay, you are *not* in a WeSpace if they are not thrilled with the impulse that you want to give.

But now, here's the great thing, we begin to confess our greatness. Confess the impulse of the Creator within us saying *Yes*.

That's a confession of greatness.

This is the social environment we can co-create:

- To share genius
- To join our creativity, our love, our oneness
- To actually *be* the impulse of the politics of Evolutionary Love at a planetary scale that has never existed before

MOVING FROM LONELINESS TO LOVING

Let's really come home now. Because home is when:

- We're awake
- We're alive
- We're in Eros

Eros is the experience of radical aliveness, moving towards contact and creativity.

Let us feel the Eros of the Cosmos, awake and alive in us.

We all have a sacred autobiography, and our sacred autobiography is a sacred text of our lives—not a narcissistic text but a text that connects us to the larger field.

I, Marc Gafni, have a story I want to tell as a parable. It must have been 25 years ago. I am leaving my house, the State of Israel has asked me to do a little lecture tour in Scandinavia. I'm 24 or 25. I'm doing my lecture tour, and I'm so excited to be doing this lecture tour, and I'm convinced that the entire future fate of the world hinges on me getting every word right and every lecture going perfectly.

As I leave the house, my son, he says, *Abba.* He says, *Dad, take this with you.*

I say, *Sure, Eytan, I'll take it with me.*

And he says, *Take a look.*

I say, *Sure.*

I put it in a box, and into this bag of books that I carry with me everywhere. In three weeks, I arrive home. It's midnight. I walk into our little apartment in Jerusalem, and Eytan is wide awake. He usually waits till the next morning to see me. As I walk in, he looks at me, and I look at him.

And—*oh my god!* At the bottom of my bag of books, I had this box he had given me. It had been this incredibly intense couple of weeks, seventeen hours a day, and I hadn't looked at the box. And he looks at me, he has a little tear running down his cheek. And I felt like it wasn't even worth being born.

I say, *Eytan!* And in Hebrew, *efshar o'chance: can I have another chance?* He imperceptibly nods, as another tear rolls down his cheek.

I go, grab the box, and open it. In the box, there's a door handle from our first apartment in Jerusalem, a silver Cross pen that I used to write with, a picture of his mother from the Palm Beach newspaper, a rock, and a seashell.

I say, Eytan, *mah zeh*? In Hebrew, *mah zeh tavim eh'lu*: Eytan, *what is this?*

Eytan says, *Abba! That's my stuff. I gave it to you; you didn't receive it.*

Like, wow! So, he was totally my teacher.

We all have a box, and in that box is *our stuff.*

- ◆ It's not our status.
- ◆ It's not our egoic structure.
- ◆ It's certainly not our bank account.
- ◆ It's not any of our degrees.

It's *our stuff.*

It's our *Hallelujah.*

It's the dreams that we lived and the dreams that are unlived.

It's the person we married and the person we didn't marry.

It's the poem only we could write.

It's the song only we could sing.

It's that unique story.

It's not your fingerprint. If you will, it's your *soul print*.

You know what it means to be lonely, my friends? To be lonely is to be unable to share your soul print with another person.

And you know why?

Well, sometimes because there's no one to receive it, that's true. Other times, we don't quite know how to express it. But those two are not usually the reason, my friends.

The reason we're lonely is because we don't know what it is. We don't know what our soul print is. If you don't have it, you can't share it. Or, even deeper, our sense of our soul print is not equal to the full depth of our power, to the full depth of our love.

We don't have a story of our lives which is equal to our love and equal to our yearning.

LOVING IS THE FUNDAMENTAL DRIVER OF REALITY

Reality is a movement from loneliness to loving, all the way up and all the way down. The first quarks, which come together to form hadrons, are joined together, they are lonely.

We have scripture on this. The entire first chapter, the Book of Genesis: *And God saw that it was good. And it was good, and it was good, and it was good, and it was good—praise!* All of the first chapter—and then in the second chapter of the Book of Genesis, that great mystical mythic text, all of the *It was good* of chapter one is nullified by a divine literary flick of the wrist, which says in the only form in the entire biblical canon, *lo tov*: *it's not good*. So, God who was good is not good.

What's not good?

Lo tov heyot ha-adam le'vado: It's not good for the human being to be lonely.

Wow!

You won the lottery. What's the first thing you do when you win the lottery? You just won the lottery! Somebody? You just won! Wow, it's awesome. You run to the phone to tell someone.

So, imagine *there is no one to tell*; there's no one to call. You remember that saying: *If a tree falls in a forest and there's no one there to hear it, does it make a sound?* If something happens to me, and there's no interiority, there is no one who receives my soul print to receive it, did it happen?

But this, *it is not good for the human being to be alone,* is not limited to human beings, my friends.

Quarks don't want to be alone.

Molecules don't want to be alone.

Cells don't want to be alone.

Actually, all the way up and all the way down the evolutionary chain is the movement beyond loneliness to loving, beyond alienation to connection, beyond separation to integration, to synergistic larger and larger wholes.

Evolution is the story of Reality moving from loneliness to loving.

Wow!

And you know what the essence of loneliness is, my friends? *I am stuck in myself.*

See, it's not enough to share my story. I have to have a story equal to my love, equal to my yearning. And my yearning, my love, is:

- I want to know Reality.
- I want to give to Reality.
- I want to imprint Reality with my unique gift.
- I want to move out of my perspective, and hear and feel you, and be delighted.
- I want to move from a politics of rage to a politics of love, from a politics of fear to a politics of empathy.

We say it is not politically correct; it is spiritually incorrect.

We want to be an Outrageous Lover.

We can't move from loneliness to loving if our love is only going to be ordinary love. Ordinary love is a strategy of the ego, security, comfort. They're beautiful, they're good. Maslow level one, level two, it's great. But it's not going to take me home.

It's only when I awaken as an Outrageous Lover and I know that I have Outrageous Acts of Love to give, that we are filled with *telos and Eros together.*

I become a *telerotic* being. I become an Evolutionary Lover. I'm giving my gift.

I'm intimately sharing with a partner or partners who are with me, giving our gifts, and I know *I am needed by All-That-Is*. Then, I am not alone.

When I know my need is Reality's need, and that all of Reality intended me, because that's the implication of a politics of Evolutionary Love. My Unique Self, my irreducibly unique expression of the LoveIntelligence and LoveBeauty of All-That-Is, is intended by All-That-Is.

Reality intended us.

Reality needs us.

Reality desires us.

How do we know Reality desires us? Because Reality only manifests what it desires.

Wow!

And all of a sudden, we have liberated desire.

Desire is not limited to the sexual; the sexual *models* the holy.

We are desired by Reality itself. That's when we are liberated from loneliness—only in an evolutionary context.

We confess our greatness, because our greatness is the gift that we have to give.

THE NEXT BUDDHA IS A *SANGHA*

What does it mean to actually come together to create a whole that's larger than the sum of its parts?

We delight in each other. So delightful, such honor, such devotion. We get to be *excited* about each other. **We get to be *devoted* to each other.** We get to move beyond the kind of commodification of Spirit, which becomes another product.

We want to *live* Spirit.

We want to *be* Spirit.

We want to *be* Outrageous.

We want to *be* spiritually incorrect.

Imagine you're living near Bethlehem, and it's the beginning of the new era, the new millennium. Are you going to Jerusalem to parties? Or are you coming because there's a new word that's being spread?

But back then it was *one person*. It's no longer one person. The next Buddha is a *sangha*. It's all of us.

We are the *sangha*.

We are the Christ Field.

We are the Evolutionary Love Field.

And there's no one extra who's here.

In deep prayer, we bow.

In deep prayer, we conclude.

We are imperfect vessels for the light. The light flows through us, we are *it* together.

We are the *sangha* together.

Let's hold our discomfort.

Let's comfort the afflicted.

Let's afflict the comfortable.

Let's be spiritually incorrect.

Let's be holy Outrageous Lovers.

CHAPTER SEVEN

THE LIBERATION FROM LONELINESS IS THE LIBERATION OF DESIRE

Episode 7 — December 17, 2016

THE WAY OF THE NEW HUMAN

We reflect on the Christmas season, so let us feel the Christ child within each of us, ready to be born. It is as if we are Mary, finding a manger, giving birth to a new human and a new humanity in the silence of the darkness, being the womb of evolution.

In this same sacred space of evolutionary receptivity was born a being who was a new human: Christ, who also held the qualities we are cultivating, as a manger for the new human within each of us.

What is the evolutionary way of the new human?

- ◆ To love your neighbor as yourself.
- ◆ To love the unique expression of divine beingness within yourself.
- ◆ To love another with the divine self coming forth from you as a gift.

- To realize the divine gift of creativity and love is God within you, is the Christ within you.

When you see your full potential self, you are seeing the God within you.

To give your gift of unique creativity to others is a giant step in overcoming loneliness. You are not alone when you are giving your gift to others in a way that is nourishing them and you.

The companion step is to receive the gift from others with passionate appreciation for their divine uniqueness.

You are never alone when loving the gifts of others.

To give and receive each other's gifts of genius is a way to Evolutionary Love, a way to shine the light at the God within each of us as expressions of unique God-given Divinity.

To give our gifts is to confess our greatness to each other.

We join our gifts. We let our gifts chime. We let our gifts shine.

THE UNIVERSE: A LOVE STORY

It is in the turning to and the turning away, it is the way we look at each other where everything happens, it is the realization that we live in a world of outrageous pain, and the only response to outrageous pain is Outrageous Love.

- We live in a world of outrageous pain. The only response to outrageous pain is Outrageous Love.
- We live in a world of outrageous beauty. The only response to outrageous beauty is Outrageous Love.

The principle is Outrageous Love, is Evolutionary Love, is the realization that *the Universe is a Love Story.*

That is the most important meme we can share.

Evolution is a story about love in action.

Evolution is not an exterior process happening out there.

Evolution *feels*.

The Universe *feels*.

The Universe *feels* love.

Love is not hard to find.

Love is impossible to avoid.

Evolutionary Love drives the entire process.

We are reclaiming what God means. We are reclaiming love. We are reclaiming what a church or a synagogue or a mosque might mean, at a higher level of consciousness.

God in the first person:

- In the Holy Trinity there is God, or love, in the first-person.
- God in the first person, which is *Tat tvam asi:* Thou Art That.
- But, not as our Eastern friends say, *Thou art awareness.*
- Rather, *Thou art love.*

God in the first person is:

Thou art a unique expression of LoveIntelligence and LoveBeauty that is the initiating and animating energy—the Eros of All-That-Is—that lives in you, as you, and through you.

Thou art unique love.

That is God, or love, in the first person.

God in the third person:

- God, or love, in the third person is that the story of evolution is love in action.

- God, or love, in the third person is the Evolutionary Love that drives the entire process of creation, which is the heart of existence itself.

Evolutionary Love and Outrageous Love are the same thing.

It is not ordinary love, a strategy of the ego.

Outrageous Love is the heart of existence itself, or the third-person love that is the driving force of everything.

God in the second person:

- Finally, we go into prayer, getting to God in the second person.
- God in the second person is God, or love, that knows your name. *You. You. You!*

FROM THE INFINITY OF POWER TO THE INFINITY OF INTIMACY

I want to ask everyone to shut their eyes for just a moment, because there are certain things you can only see with your eyes shut.

When we shut our eyes, we open the inner eye. We step into God in the third person, we step into love that drives *all* of Reality.

Imagine billions of light years, cosmic creativity in every moment, the entire table of complex elements in chemistry, all the laws of physics. Imagine the infinite power of Reality that all the great traditions understood, the supernovas of Divinity exploding all through the evolutionary chain in dazzling intelligence beyond imagination.

No supercomputer, no team of supercomputers, no artificial intelligence can even bear the pale glimmer of what is the infinite power and intelligence of Source that animates all of Reality.

That is God in love in the third person.

That is the Infinity of Power over those billions of light years.

Imagine that. Feel it. Touch into it.

Then, move from the Infinity of Power to the Infinity of Intimacy, knowing that all of that energy, love, power, and intelligence is **the third person of God sitting in a chair next to you, knowing your name, caring about you, desperately yearning about your life.**

Know that your entire life is dignified, needed, honored, and recognized, and that your entire life is *Hallelujah*.

THE HOLY AND THE BROKEN HALLELUJAH

In every moment, whether it is a *holy or a broken Hallelujah*, from my lips, She (Goddess) is drawing *Hallelujah*. [*See Appendix.*]

> *Hallelujah* in Hebrew, *hallel*—praise, pristine praise.

> *Hallelujah, holelut*—the drunken intoxication when we are lost in life.

In every moment, life is a holy and a broken Hallelujah!

Hallelujah speaks, as King David did, of the dignity of our lives.

Our lives are infinitely dignified.

Our lives are adequate.

Our lives are needed.

- We don't want to move *beyond* our story.

- We want to move beyond our *ego* story, or the story of our contraction.
- We want to enter into the story of our *Unique Self* or our sacred autobiography, where we realize that my love story is part of *The Universe: A Love Story*.

The great principle is The Universe: A Love Story, an *Evolutionary Love Story*.

My personal love story is not my contraction. It is not my way of handling my early attachment issues. It is not my way of covering over the emptiness.

No.

My love story is the Universe having a me experience.

It is *The Universe: A Love Story*, uniquely as me.

A STORY ABOUT PRAYER: ASK FOR EVERYTHING!

We have received so many beautiful emails from people saying: *Wow, I thought prayer was a fundamentalist thing.*

We realized, no, the god you don't believe in doesn't exist, not a fundamentalist god, who is ethnocentric, homophobic, owned by one church.

No.

It is the personal face of Essence that knows my name. What the Hindus and the Jews called the Mother. Mother, *Eema*: Mother, who holds me.

Feel into that and say, *what do we ask Mother for?*

A holy story. There is a master called Israel, the *Baal Shem Tov*, the Master of the Good Name, the founder of the Hasidic movement. He goes on this trip with his disciples. They get to a town—a hamlet in Russia. They knock at a door and ten pious disciples walk in with the *Baal Shem Tov* to a very poor family.

The wife is like: *Oh my god, we barely have food for the week, we have to feed these people?*

But, the husband says, *Yes, whatever they'd like.*

So the *Baal Shem Tov*, this Master of the Good Name, says, *Give me the biggest breakfast in the world.*

His disciples are all ashamed. *Biggest breakfast? This is a poor man, why are you asking for the biggest breakfast in the world?*

He says, *give me the biggest breakfast.*

So, the poor family gives the Master of the Good Name the biggest breakfast in the world.

The disciples hope they are leaving, but they all stay for lunch and the master says, *Give me the biggest lunch in the world, everything. Slaughter your chickens, whatever you have.* (This was pre-vegetarian age. Whole Foods wasn't around. Slaughter!)

The disciples want to get the heck out of there. Their master is totally embarrassing them. This family is so poor and the master just asked for the biggest lunch for all ten of us.

The master says, *I'm staying for dinner as well.*

Are you serious, ask the disciples, *we're staying for dinner? This poor man has nothing.*

We're staying for dinner. I'd like you to make me the biggest dinner around as a meal to God.

The disciples think he's gone crazy. They knew he was a crazy wisdom master. They can't believe it. He's gone crazy. He eats dinner. He gobbles everything up.

The disciples are forced to eat by their master. They leave completely ashamed. Six of the disciples leave their master because he's obviously gone crazy, two refuse to talk to him, and two show up the rest of the year, but are completely alienated and disillusioned.

A year goes by.

On exactly that date the master says, *Let's go visit them again.*

Oh my god, say the two disciples, *Let's go visit them again, are you serious?*

They do travel. Lions and tigers and bears, oh my!

They get to this hamlet in eastern Russia. They come before this man's home, which was dilapidated, poor, and broken down. There is a miniature palace and this beautiful gate on the outside. There are horses. They walk in. There are servants and light shining.

The master says to the man, this poor man who is now obviously not poor at all and is now living in this beautiful home, the master says: *Please, tell my disciples what happened!*

So the man says, *When you left last time, I had nothing. You had taken everything I had. I went into the forest. I had always prayed to God for all— the whole world but never for me because I didn't want to bother God. At this point, I had seven children and my wife; you had taken everything from me. I was furious, so I had no choice.*

I turned to God and I said, God, you've got to help me! I am going to tell you exactly what I need! I need money for this week. I need this for my children. For the first time, I just asked for everything.

I asked for everything.

Then, a particular business deal came my way, then something else, then something else, my entire fortune began to turn.

The master said: *When you pray—listen to this man—you ask for everything.*

111

HOLY PRAYERS OF THE COMMUNITY

Ask for everything!

Ask for the people in Aleppo, who are desperate for the world to intervene.

Ask for your uncle Morris, who needs to have surgery.

Ask for your own creativity.

Ask for your relationships.

Prayer is what removes us from loneliness.

Prayer liberates us.

We know we may live lives, occasionally, of quiet desperation, but we are never lonely. We are never alone.

We turn to the Divine, and we say, *Help me!*

Help me!

So I ask everybody—write your prayers, and let's reclaim prayer. Prayer, not to the fundamentalist god but prayer to the God-who-knows-our-name, who is the Source of All, who is *the force of the second person*. God who is Evolutionary Love, God who is holding us in the world.

Let's reclaim prayer. Take the time. The gates are open, and everything can go in.

Everything can be opened up. Let's hear your prayers:

- ◆ D: *I pray to always be the best version of ourselves.*
- ◆ E: *I pray for a new baby.*
- ◆ C: *I pray for my grandchildren to have wonderful lives of Outrageous Love.*
- ◆ K: *I pray for all of us to live as love-in-action.*
- ◆ E: *I pray for all the Syrians. I pray for the indigenous beings of the world.*

Pray for everyone.

Prayer affirms the dignity of personal needs.

If I can't affirm the dignity of my own personal need, I can't recognize the dignity of someone else's personal need.

Are we evangelical? Yes, we are! This is good news. The good news of knowing that we are held.

Let the prayers open up the gates of Heaven.

Let's pray for everyone.

I pray for all the people of Aleppo, who are reaching out to the world and saying *help us!* I pray for Donald Trump to open his eyes, and Barack Obama to open his eyes. Both of them—to come together and speak and say—we are going to step into Aleppo. **We are going to stop the suffering. For the first time in the twentieth and twenty-first centuries, we are not going to allow that kind of pain—outrageous pain—to happen in front of us.**

Pray and don't forget. Don't skip yourself. If you skip yourself, your prayer doesn't open.

Prayer affirms the dignity of personal need.

A CALL TO ACTION FOR *HOMO AMOR UNIVERSALIS*

This is an outrageous prayer that goes with Outrageous Love.

Pray that everyone on Earth *feels it* as their *unique impulse* to give *their* love, to create with one another.

Ask everyone on Earth to join together in prayer and love, in a planetary awakening, before the greatest catastrophes that are foreseen to happen.

Ask to be one of the nurturing places, one of the wellsprings for those who want to give their love to co-create a world equal to our spiritual, social, and scientific potentials.

Be part of such a loving community.

You have within you a love so big, so great, and so large that you don't know what to do with it. Just let it all out because you can!

Is that okay? Is it okay to be just as loving as you could possibly be with each other?

Give birth together like Mary with the Christ child in the manger. Each of us is the Christ child in the manger.

We have to *come out* and be loved!

What kind of human can handle all this power of nanotech, biotech, quantum computing, thermonuclear bombs? Who is great enough to handle all this power? You—all of you—who are desirous and ready are the way! **Be beacons of light unto yourselves.**

Be a tiny band—a brave congregation of souls attracted to the future of the world—be avant-garde.

We are attracted to the future of the world. We don't know fully what it is, but we are capable of being attracted.

You are a new order of the future!

You are self-selected souls, who have come to Earth to carry the miracle of the resurrection into action, as the transformation of humanity from *Homo sapiens sapiens* to *Homo universalis*.

The species that can use all the powers that science and technology have given to us, with love, is a new humanity.

Receive from the evolutionary consciousness of Christ. We are right at the threshold of that being born. Send us all out, a place of home to be.

A call for the avant-garde of humanity.

- Activate the capacity to save the world from self-destruction.
- Undertake a mission comparable to the first disciples. They were the first to carry the message of the Reality of our potentials to all the nations.

You will do the work that I do, and greater works than these will you do, said Christ.

You are the last to carry this message. They lived at the beginning of the change. You are living at the end times of this phase of evolution.

True? This text is a call to action to new disciples of Christ and all great spiritual masters—to manifest their own capacity to do as Christ did and more. The text is for the avant-garde of humanity, those who awaken with love in their hearts and joy in their spirits, as the glory that shall be revealed in all of us.

I call upon *Homo universalis*. Those in whom the flame of expectation burns high. **With love in your hearts, yes, we call upon *Homo universalis* to set about the double task of self-transformation and the activation of the world's capacities to achieve the goal of its history.**

A *Yes* to self-evolution, and to the evolution of the world as one connected action.

The evolutionary *Yes*, the holy *Yes*! We are to become *natural Christs*.

We are to communicate to the world its potential to restore the Earth, to free the people, and to impregnate the universe with new life.

We are *Homo universalis*, or *Homo amor*.

We are here to participate in the world. We live in a participatory universe. When enough people feel empathy for each other, for nature, for Spirit… because we are here to participate in instances of cooperation, in the planetary birth, in the second coming of Christ in all of us.

NURTURE THE GENIUS OF HUMANITY IN US

This is our purpose: to nurture the genius of humanity within every one of us and to confess our greatness to the world, so that the greatness of every person can be received.

The massive feeling of loneliness, which is considered to be one of the most painful of the psychological problems in the modern Western world, can only be overcome by giving our gifts of love the whole way.

Outrageous Love is not ordinary love; it is Evolutionary Love.

A little story. I, Barbara, was once at the Mount Calvary Monastery, doing communion everyday with those monks—holy, holy communion, eating, taking the Body of Christ. We were these poor, sacred strangers, lost.

So, I finally went up to one of these priests, and I said to the monk in the beautiful white robes and all of that, *I don't feel like a poor, sacred, lost stranger. Do you?*

He said, *Of course not, it is just poetry!*

I said, *It is bad poetry!*

Let's write new poetry. Not our sin. We must confess our greatness.

I went to that monastery for a long while, but then I stopped going and I started to do the communion all by myself and I began to recognize that I can consciously consume the living Body of Christ, comparable to what the nuns do when they take the Eucharist.

The Eucharist is an enormously potent ritual. It is not a ritual. It is an actuality. Because all those hundreds of thousands of nuns worldwide are consuming every single day—the frequency of that living body.

Give our gifts of love to each other. Once those gifts can be given, nothing will ever take them back again—we will never be alone again.

THE ONLY RESPONSE TO OUTRAGEOUS PAIN IS OUTRAGEOUS LOVE

Amen! Amen! In this moment, we bring in all those people from Aleppo. They are with us.

We confess our greatness and devote ourselves to the higher evolutionary cause.

It was Patti Smith singing at the Nobel Prize Award Ceremony, Bob Dylan's "A Hard Rain's A-Gonna Fall."

> *Where have you been, my blue-eyed son?*
>
> *Where have you been, my darling young one?*
>
> *I stumbled on the side of 12 misty mountains.*
>
> *I've walked, I've crawled on six crooked highways.*
>
> *I've stepped in the middle of seven sad forests.*
>
> *I've been out in front of a dozen dead oceans.*
>
> *I've been 10,000 miles in the mouth of a graveyard.*
>
> *And it's a hard, it's a hard, it's a hard.*
>
> *It's a hard rain's a-gonna fall.*

It is a story of outrageous pain.

> *I saw a newborn baby with wild wolves all around.*
>
> *I saw a highway of diamonds with nobody on it.*
>
> *I saw a black branch with blood that kept dripping.*
>
> *I saw a roomful of men with their hammers a-bleedin'.*
>
> *I saw a white ladder all covered with water.*
>
> *I saw 10,000 talkers whose tongues were all broken.*

117

I saw guns and sharp swords in the hands of young children.

We want to hold the outrageous pain.

We are going to move it into Outrageous Love.

Speaking, praying, for Aleppo, inviting Donald Trump. Donald Trump as an Outrageous Lover. Barack Obama as an Outrageous Lover.

You know, when we wrote a tweet a couple of weeks ago, *Donald Trump is an Outrageous Lover*—a particular reporter, who is not a fan of mine, retweeted it: *Oh my god! How could Marc Gafni say Donald Trump is an Outrageous Lover?*

You know what? If we demonize Donald Trump, then Donald Trump is going to be a demon. **When we demonize people, they become demons.**

But, when we look at people and say, *you are an Outrageous Lover*, then their natural true essence emerges, whether that is Sarah Palin, or Michelle Obama, or Barack Obama, or Bill Clinton, or Hillary Clinton, or Donald Trump. America has got to be sacred because we always seek transformation.

We've got to come together.

We are not against each other.

We are against un-love.

We live in a world of outrageous pain—Bob Dylan sings of outrageous pain—now we are going to take it to Outrageous Love.

Yes, we are excited! We say every week, we are evangelicals. We are bringing the good news.

The good news of Outrageous Love.

The good news of evolution.

The good news that evolution awakens in us, as person and in person.

Outrageous pain always comes from the feeling that I am alone.

Outrageous pain comes from loneliness.

Outrageous pain comes from pseudo-eros, the addictions, the addictions to power.

The addictions to power always disguise themselves. You know, in the church, the Borgias, the Popes, they were doing all the rituals, but they were still addicted to power.

Sometimes in the New Age movement or the Human Potential movement, we have people addicted to their activism. It is worldcentric consciousness. It is an egocentric psychology. **We can talk about the world making peace, but we don't know how to make peace ourselves. We have to make peace among us.**

We have to be the change—said Gandhi—*that we want to bring to the world.*

FOUR NOBLE TRUTHS

Let's go deep for a second. What are our noble truths?

- The first noble truth: you are an irreducibly unique expression of LoveIntelligence. You are a Unique Self.
- The second noble truth: Uniqueness tells you that Reality intended you. Feel that! You can actually feel what they call in Buddhism—*kensho*. You step out of yourself. Reality intended you.
- The third noble truth: Reality not only intended you, Reality *desires* you. Wow, Reality desires you!

We usually associate the word desire with the sexual. Now desire in the sexual is beautiful. But what we've done is —

We have exiled desire to the sexual.

119

Since we have exiled desire to the sexual, and since there is a basic human need to be desired, the sexual collapses under the weight of a burden it cannot bear.

We turn every sexual issue into an insult, then we wind up:

- With sexual abuse
- With sexual harassment
- With false complaints
- With rape
- With the weaponizing of sex

Look at the election we just had. Bill Clinton sitting in the front row. Donald Trump brings in people who accuse Bill Clinton. Donald Trump getting accused by ten other people.

Weaponizing sex.

What about holding a holy world? A holy world in which desire is holy.

The sexual is so confused because we look to the sexual as the affirmation that we are desired, which is the exile of the holy into the sexual.

The sexual has to *model* the holy, not *be* the holy.

Where does desire live?

Desire is the very nature of Reality.

Desire is the *knowing* that you are desired by *all of Reality*.

The implication of uniqueness, of being a *Unique Self*, is that Reality desires you.

Reality only manifests what it desires. Reality is allurement and desire, all the way up and all the way down, from quarks becoming hadrons, leptons, muons, subatomic particles, up through molecules and cells.

Evolutionary Love is another word for desire.

The entire evolutionary process is Evolutionary Love.

It is desire, all the way up and all the way down.

To be a human being, say the great evolutionary mystics in the original scripture, *hakadosh baruch hu mit'aveh la'asot dirato, ba'tachtonim*; God desires you. You are desired by God.

Wow, we are desired by God!

That is not a myth.

It is not a metaphor.

It is sanity.

It is the truth of Reality.

Your uniqueness implies that Reality, through massive sets of holy synchronicities, desired your existence. The Universe is having a *you* experience; the Universe desires a you experience.

Finally, the fourth holy truth: You are needed by All-That-Is. Reality *needs* you.

Reality needs your service.

Reality needs your gift.

Reality needs your unique creativity.

Remember, when you imagine Barack Obama, President of the United States of America, calls you up and says, *I can't believe it. I've been watching you, and you are it, you are it!* He knows all about you. He describes your unique talents, and exactly what you know and how you do it, everything about you. Then he says: *what you have is needed by All-That-Is.*

You get off the phone. How do you feel? Depressed? Do you run for your Prozac? Do you run to take another New Age course? I don't think so.

Everything has literally shifted within.

You are ecstatic.

You realize, *oh my god—I am needed!*

THE LIBERATION FROM LONELINESS IS THE LIBERATION OF DESIRE

Wow, the liberation from loneliness! You cannot be liberated from loneliness by just having one other person that you tell all your stuff to all the time. That is just the beginning.

Of course, you want to share all your stuff. But, to be liberated from loneliness, you have to know:

- Reality knows your name.
- Reality loves you.
- Reality desires you.
- Reality needs your service.

All of a sudden, it all opens up; it all comes alive in a different way.

It is the liberation of desire.

Here is a sentence. It is the biggest sentence in the world:

---

*All failures of ethics come
from a collapse of Eros.*

Eros is the knowing that we live in *The Universe: A Love Story.*

To live an erotic life has nothing to do with sex:

- You can be celibate and live an erotic life.
- You can be polyamorous and live an erotic life.
- You can be monogamous and live an erotic life.

Eros means that you are awake with the shimmering flame of Outrageous Love, giving the unique gifts that are yours to give, that can be given by no one else but you.

Eros means to know:

There is a poem only you can write.

There is a song only you can sing.

There is a way of being, laughing, loving in the world that is desperately needed by All-That-Is that is the highest expression of Reality that only you can do to perfection, which is to be yourself.

You might as well be yourself because as Oscar Wilde said, *Everybody else is taken.*

We enter into this new evolutionary ritual, called "Confess Your Greatness." To confess your greatness is to confess something that you did, a moment you had a realization, a good act that you did.

When I confess my sin, if I am a wretch, what does the world want from me?

When you confess your greatness, we begin to become alive. We come together in Unique Self Symphony.

CONFESSIONS OF GREATNESS

Confess your greatness, saying *Yes* to the impulse of evolution to go the whole way in this lifetime, to everyone else going the whole way.

Our greatness is to catalyze a world in which each person is able to live up to their potential. Our greatness is calling us to live our potential in synchronistic synergy in time. **The pain that is everywhere can be healed by connecting our greatness worldwide.**

We are imperfect vessels for the light.

We are evangelicals.

We are bringing the good news as imperfect vessels for the light.

We are not politically correct.

We are spiritually incorrect.

We are moving from a politics of rage to a politics of love.

From a politics of fear to a politics of empathy.

To everyone who is an irreducible Unique Self in Unique Self Symphony, generating a planetary awakening in love.

CHAPTER EIGHT

OUTRAGEOUS LOVE IS A PERCEPTION

Episode 8 — December 24, 2016

THE GREAT RECONSTRUCTIVE PROJECT

It's a rare time: We are celebrating both Christmas Eve and Hanukkah eve. It's the first night of Hanukkah, the first light, the first candle of Hanukkah is lit, and we are also on Christmas Eve.

Our evolutionary movement is about:

- The evolution of Christmas,
- The evolution of Hanukkah.
- Reclaiming prayer at a higher level of consciousness.
- Not being politically correct but spiritually incorrect.

Politically correct means protecting people from all sorts of microaggressions, where we include and include and include, but we forget to include a positive image of Reality. Political correctness is, *let's protect ourselves from any and all hurt, but we have nothing positive to say.*

Politically correct *is* beautiful, but we forget to articulate a positive vision of Reality.

We are so postmodern that we've deconstructed everything. We say that *everything* is a social construction of Reality. All the deconstructions are over. We're all protected, but who are we?

What's our identity?

Where are we going?

What's the vision of our lives?

What's the larger story?

We need to begin the great reconstructive project—that reconstructive project, that new vision that incorporates the best of premodern, modern, and postmodern in a gorgeous, integral vision of love, of Evolutionary Love.

The new Evolutionary Story in which Hanukkah evolves, and Christmas evolves, and Ramadan evolves, and they integrate into a higher place— that is *spiritually incorrect.*

It's spiritually incorrect because we are saying that some things are *true* and things *matter.*

There are narratives and stories that are not just social constructions but actually reflect deep truths about Reality like:

- Reality is driven by love, or evolutionary Eros.
- Reality is moving towards more and more love.
- Evolution is love in action.

THE MIRACLE OF HANUKKAH

The word is like this:

A little bit of light dispels a lot of darkness.

A minor fluctuation point in a whole system up-levels the entire system.

The miracle of Hanukkah is the story of the Maccabees, 165 B.C.E. The temple in Jerusalem is conquered by Antiochus Epiphanes and then recaptured by the Maccabees.

They want to relight, rekindle, the menorah, but there is not enough olive oil—kosher oil— in order to rekindle. There is only enough oil for one day.

They decide to light the menorah anyways and, miracle of miracles, in this great, holy, mythic, gorgeous story, what happens? The oil lasts for eight days.

Here's the evolutionary question: If there was only enough oil for one day, in that great Hanukkah myth, but the oil lasted eight days, how long was the miracle?

Seven, right, because you had enough oil for one day. The extra days were only seven days. The miracle was only seven days, so why do we have Hanukkah for eight days?

The great evolutionary answer: **The miracle of the first day is having the courage to light the candle even though you don't have enough oil.**

That's how evolution works; evolution works in baby steps:

- We take the first step.
- We dare to light the candle.
- We dare to hope.
- We dare to dream.
- We dare to take the first step even though we have no idea how the whole journey is going to traverse.

It's the lighting of the candle itself which is the true miracle of *Hanukkah*.

Crisis is an evolutionary driver; that's the evolutionary invitation.

Now let's go into the resonance of what the *Silent Night* feels like, and listen to Sinéad O'Connor sing "Silent Night":

Silent night, holy night.

All is calm, all is bright.

Round yon Virgin, Mother and Child.

Holy infant so tender and mild, we say,

Sleep in heavenly peace,

Sleep in heavenly peace.

THE SACRED STORY OF EVOLUTION

Silent night, holy night, holy promise that was given to us at the birth of Christ. In this resonance, I would like all of us to tune into that source of being within us that is pulsing with the power and presence and being of the evolving Christ.

This impulse that we have to love more, to create more, to be more was promised to us by Christ when he said, *You will do the works that I do, and greater works than these will you do in the fullness of time.*

This *is* the fullness of time.

Why do we say, *this is the fullness of time*? Why do we believe that this is the fullness of time?

We live at the exact moment of evolution when the human species is being required to wake up, to become a guide of our own evolution. We realize we're waking up to be guides to our own evolution.

How do we know which way to guide ourselves? The guide is the sacred story of evolution. The sacred story of evolution tells us that at a time of critical breakdown we need to become aware of:

- The emergence of the new
- The higher order of consciousness
- The higher order of freedom
- The more comprehensive synergistic order

This is the promise of evolution. This is not a mystical dream of Reality. This is a scientific, psychological, and spiritual discovery.

The story of evolution is the story of the birth of the living Christ, of the living Buddha, of the living Divine in every one of us.

Our first way of knowing this is the time of the change, that this is the Evolutionary Story of creation is because **we cannot continue to live in this degree of separation and survive**.

It is also true that the precise story of the birth of Christ, as it is written in the New Testament, tells us that the time will come when *You will do the works that I do*, said He, *and greater works than these will you do, because I go to the Father.*

What does that mean? It means that *everyone* who says *Yes*:

- To the inner impulse of the Divine
- To the inner impulse of creativity
- To the inner impulse to love more, be more, do more
- To the model of the living Christ
- To the living universal human
- To the living Evolutionary Unique Self

Everyone who says *Yes* has, coded in the entire memory of our life, the knowing of the next stages of evolution for more consciousness, greater freedom, more synergistic order, and more love.

Doing the works that Jesus did, and greater works, and being the most blessed generation of humans ever to be on the face of this Earth.

Consciously—to be aware—we face devolution and destruction, or evolution and co-creation.

We place ourselves in the mind of God. 13.8 billion years ago, the Creator awoke to desire the creation.

How else could this have happened?

129

As the Creator desired the creation, He created the quarks, the electrons, the protons, the neutrons, all the way up the chain of life. Every particle is attracted to every other particle by allurement, by Eros, by attraction.

Bring that awesome journey of evolution, by attracting it to ever greater parts of a greater whole system, to bring it into our consciousness.

In our own hearts, the impulse of evolution, to more consciousness, more freedom, more order, more love. Rather than thinking this is simply an impossible dream, in this resonance, we know and declare it is the conscious direction of the entire process of creation.

By awakening together and by deepening our memory of the future growing within us, we do declare we will give birth in every one of us—

- ◆ to the natural Christ,
- ◆ to the universal human,
- ◆ to the co-creator of a new world.

ENACTING A MEMORY OF THE FUTURE

We are the memory of the future.

In much of the world of addiction, for instance, the focus is on recovering the memory of the past in order to get healthy and whole. But, when we realize the nature of Reality, we realize the reason the addiction treatments—which can be so beautiful—still have many people treatment doesn't work for is because **you can't get healthy by just recovering a memory of the past.**

We need a memory of the future. Hope is a memory of the future. Evolution is a memory of the future. Evolution is love in action. A positive vision, a reconstructive vision, a memory of the future, that is evolution in action.

Be not politically correct but spiritually incorrect, to actually claim and enact this memory of the future.

The intelligence of Reality hears our voice

To realize that the god we don't believe in doesn't exist, and that we can pray again, and that prayer is not owned by a xenophobic, regressive, homophobic, patriarchal community, or by a particular church.

Prayer is the awake, living realization that not only does the Divine live in me, but I am held in every moment.

Read Rumi. Every passage in Rumi is about: *I am the Beloved and I am falling into the arms of the Beloved. Every place I fall, I fall into God's hands.*

Christ is holding me every second.

The Mother, *Rama Krishna, Mother! Mother, Mother, hold me Mother. Rama Krishna*, the great non-dual realizer who realizes I am held by the Mother.

Divinity is, God is, the Mother is, the Ceaseless Creativity of All, alive in me even as She holds me. We turn to Her and we ask for everything because prayer affirms the dignity of personal need.

We realize that God is not only God in the third person, the Infinity of Power, billions of light years of complexity and gorgeousness, science, physics, and the laws of mathematics, but God is also second person, the Infinity of Intimacy that knows my name.

You are, I am, God's unique intimacy.

We open the gates in prayer, Leonard Cohen, modern hymn maker, *Hallelujah.*

Whatever is happening in life, *even when it all goes wrong, we stand before the Lord of Song and from our lips She draws the Hallelujah.*

Hallelujah as we know is pristine praise and *holelut*, the drunken stupor that life sometimes leaves us in. *There's a blaze of light in every word*, in *the holy and the broken Hallelujah.*

And from that place of *Hallelujah*, we turn to offer prayer. We pray our voices into the noosphere, into the resonant field. The intelligence of Reality hears our voice. That's a pointing-out instruction. That's what prayer means:

- Reality is intelligent.
- Reality manifests mitosis and meiosis, before there was a neocortex.
- Our intelligence participates in the intelligence of Reality.
- The same way that we can hear each other, Reality hears us.

It's true! It's awesome!

Reality, the god you don't believe in that doesn't exist. **It's the God who is the Infinity of Intimacy, who is the ceaseless, intelligent creativity of Cosmos that knows our name, that assures that we never live in lonely desperation because every one of our tears is drunk by God.**

When we pray, we ask for everything because prayer affirms the dignity of personal need. Let's be evangelicals, sharing the good news.

The good news is that I'm held, that I'm not alone, that the Infinity of Intimacy knows my name.

LIFE IS EVER EVOLVING

We bring the message of *life ever evolving* to the world.

We give the gift of this greater hope, greater life, greater purpose to everyone in the world, so that we can assist the world in coming together in a new faith and a new discipline of hope.

In 1980, I [Barbara Marx Hubbard] had a first Christ experience. I was trying to write a book on the future of humanity, and I asked the Universe a question: *What kind of person can handle all the power of science, technology, biology?*

I had been working with Jonas Salk, and he showed me the biolabs that people were working in. On the door of the lab was, *Stamp out physical death*. This would be a large step forward, if we were to stamp out physical death.

We don't know what it means. And if we add nanotech, biotech, quantum computing, artificial intelligence, which is all already happening, we are at the stage of being able to do the works that Jesus did, and even greater works.

Within our lifetime, if we can bring the new power of gods the human race has created by the intelligence we have been given, we could experience the breakthrough of the system, rather than experiencing the breakdown.

Together.

We could experience, in the language of Teilhard de Chardin, the noosphere getting its collective eyes, where everyone places any gift into the thinking layer of Earth, our voices, our words, our passion coming right into the thinking layer of Earth.

Our goal, just like for the Catholics, is the second coming of Christ, **the first awakening of humanity as one creative body born into a universe of infinite intelligence and life.**

It could be right in our lifetime, even in the next few years! We could have a disastrous decline. The timing is exactly like the timing of a birth. The timing of birth is once that labor pain starts you can't say, I think I'll go on a walk or go to the store. This is true of the birth of humanity at this time of crises.

Humanity, we're in it together.

In asking what kind of person could handle the new powers, I [Barbara] got an image of the living Christ. I was walking by a monastery. I saw hang gliders jumping off a high mountain with butterfly-colored wings.

They descended above the cross, and the image of mass metamorphosis occurred to me.

Behold, I show you mysteries, said Saint Paul. *We shall not all sleep, we shall all be changed, in a moment, in the twinkling of an eye, at the last trump. And the trumpet shall sound.*

I thought, oh my god, **the meaning of the resurrection is the metamorphosis of humanity**.

You will do the works that I did, and greater works will you do, in the fullness of time, He told us. I have a whole workbook from this writing. I want to read a section:

> *Jesus Christ was simply a first example of what you can all be.*
>
> *Since very few could actualize their full potential during the last two thousand years, I was deified and put above you all. People worshiped me instead of actualizing themselves. My mission was to trigger the awareness that you are all to become joint heirs with Christ. You shall do the works that I did and even greater works shall you do.*
>
> *Now is the time in planetary history when the hidden human reserve will be triggered in millions and millions of you at once.*
>
> *Your biochemical systems are being stimulated by Holy Love.*
>
> *Esoterically, from without, the noosphere, the thinking layer of Earth is thickening, linking everyone in an information plenum in which we, of the new resurrection of humanity, are putting our input into right now, into this noosphere.*
>
> *Esoterically, from within, the evolutionary spiritual adepts are triggering God-consciousness and mind/body transformation by conscious choice to attend to the presence of the inner Divinity.*

Folks, is this true? Yes, yes, yes!

We are here for the planetary awakening of humanity. It will happen in our lifetime. We are in service to that great mission. Each of us is going to incarnate the living Christ, by the effort to do this.

OUTRAGEOUS LOVE IS A PERCEPTION

A prayer of Christmas, on Hanukkah eve, is "I Want To Know What Love Is," by Foreigner. What does it mean to be rooted not in ordinary love but in Outrageous Love? Just like in that time in Bethlehem, we are the people. It's our turn, in this generation. We are the ones who want to know what love is.

We are here together. We are Christ in the manger. We want to know what love is, not ordinary love but Outrageous Love.

We live in a world of outrageous pain, the only response to outrageous pain is Outrageous Love.

We live in a world of outrageous beauty, the only response to outrageous beauty is Outrageous Love.

What is the difference between Outrageous Love and ordinary love?

Ordinary love is a strategy of the ego. Ordinary love is an emotion, energy in motion, a reaction.

Outrageous Love is a perception.

I [Marc] was sitting with the Dalai Lama in his sitting room in Dharamsala. We were talking about love. We were sharing the difference between Buddhist deep teachings and Hebraic/Kabbalah deep teachings. I shared with him this simple, beautiful idea that love, at its core, is not an emotion, it's a perception. He got so excited, one of the wonderful things about the Dalai Lama is that he gets excited. He gets excited, and he starts jumping up and down going, *Beautiful, beautiful, beautiful*, in that great way that he does.

Emily Dickinson said, *Not revelation 'tis that waits, but our unvarnished eyes.*

We have to *unvarnish* our eyes.

We have to cleanse the doors of perception.

An emotion comes and goes.

A perception gets infinitely deeper.

To be a lover is to see with the eyes of God.

If love is a perception, then we can all become lovers. Love doesn't wane away or fall away after five years, or ten. It gets deeper and deeper.

Here's the evolutionary vision of a holiday: A holiday is a holy day. A holy day is when we are lovers. To be lovers is to see with God's eyes. To be lovers is: We're not waiting for the redemption, it's already here.

The great Christian contribution to the prophetic conversation of redemption is that Christ has already come. He's already here.

And then the Jews said back, *Yes, Christ is already here, and we have to bring Him.* We have to transform; we have to create heaven on Earth; we have to bring those two visions of redemption together, and we get the heavenly vision.

Christ is already here; it's already true.

Remember Jerry Maguire? Tom Cruise said, *I love him not for the man he is but for the man he almost is* or *for the man he wants to be.* That's not it. That's ordinary love.

Outrageous Love is when I look at you in my gaze and you already *are transformed.* **When I look at you, you are transformed.**

Wow! Can you feel that?

We tweeted something, we wrote, *Trump is an Outrageous Lover.* A bunch of reporters retweeted it. How could they say something so terrible?

Then we tweeted, *Hillary Clinton is an Outrageous Lover* and yes *Sarah Palin is an Outrageous Lover. Michelle Obama is an Outrageous Lover and Barack Obama. Bill Clinton is an Outrageous Lover.*

What does it mean when I actually look at a person and I don't demonize them?

It's not that I am not careful, it's not that I don't tie my camel to a post, it's not that I don't fight for the environment, of course I should.

But instead of saying, *he's the other*:

- How much of this country made Hillary Clinton the other?
- How much of this country made Donald Trump the other?
- We demonize the other and then *we* get to be kosher.
- When we don't feel like we're really in the circle, we put somebody else outside the circle to give us the *illusion* that we are on the inside.

That is not Eros, that is pseudo-eros.

To be a lover is to see with God's eyes and to know that it's already true.

A holy day is a day when it's already true.

We love Christmas because we see a little clearer. Our hearts are a little softer. Scrooge is in our ear.

We're lighting the *menorah.*

The light is already here.

We know that just a little bit of light dispels so much darkness.

AN EVOLUTIONARY STORY ABOUT A MASTER

Here is what we call an Evolutionary Story. It's a beautiful, mystical story about a master who lived in the place where Jesus lived, in Safed, in Israel.

He was a great master. It was about 1790. He had come from Europe. When he decided to move to Israel, a man came into his study hall and whispered in his ear. This whisper in his ear moves him, a divine whisper. He moves his entire mystical court to Israel, to Safed, that place near Tiberius, near the Great Sea, where Jesus walked.

He's there for thirty years, and he develops his community, until thirty years later that same man in Europe who had whispered in his ear walks again into the study hall. The man whispers in his ear again, and his face goes white.

He steps out of the public room, goes into his private room, and he refuses to see anyone. He *refuses* to see anyone. They all see him staring out of the window at the cobblestone streets of Safed for seven days. All he does is stare.

Then, seven days later he comes out, and he jumps on the tables of the study hall. He begins to dance, and all of the disciples begin to dance with him. Oh my god, lions and tigers and bears, oh my, ecstasy!

They dance all night, and when they fall exhausted at dawn, one of the older disciples says, *Nu voos tutuzchik* in Yiddish, meaning, *what just happened? Who was that man who came thirty years ago that we remember?* And he just came again. *What did he say in your ear?*

The master says, *Thirty years ago when that man whispered in my ear he said, "Go to the Holy Land. In the Holy Land the air is more pure than the air of heaven. The water is more clear and gorgeous than the water of the Garden of Eden. The stones, the cobblestones in Safed, are diamonds and rubies."*

I came here to Israel. The air was more pure than the air of heaven. The water was more clean and clear, crystal and gorgeous, and refreshing and life-giving than even the water of the Garden of Eden. But the stones, the cobblestones, were just cobblestones. They weren't diamonds and rubies. It wasn't true. He exaggerated.

Then the man came thirty years later whispering in my ear, and he said, *The cobblestones ARE diamonds and rubies*, and I realized I couldn't see.

If I couldn't see, it means I didn't love enough. I didn't love enough.

I spent seven days finding all the love inside of me until just a few hours ago I looked at the cobblestones, and there it was; they were diamonds and rubies. It was true! It was true!

To be a lover is to open our eyes, to know that it's already here, that the Christ child is already born, that it's our turn, that we can make a difference, that we can change everything.

Yes, whenever a new life force arises there will be attempts to murder all life forces and all social forces.

Again, I'm going to say, *Donald Trump is an Outrageous Lover.* I'm madly in love with him. Sarah Palin is an Outrageous Lover. I am madly in love with her. I am filled with admiration, and I am in devotion. Bill Clinton is an Outrageous Lover and Hillary, Outrageous Lover. Michelle, oh my god, an Outrageous Lover. We are each Outrageous Lovers.

Outrageous Love is not a mere human emotion, it's the heart of existence itself.

Forgive me my dear friends, forgive us, we always ask you to forgive us because we get so caught up. We're all wounded healers; we're all imperfect vessels for the light. But, most of all, we're messengers who forgot the message.

- ◆ We are the message.
- ◆ We are the future.
- ◆ In each other's gaze, we become whole, and we become holy.

CHAPTER NINE

RECLAIMING GOD AS EVOLUTION: BEYOND THE EXILE OF EVOLUTION TO TECHNOLOGY

Episode 9 — December 31, 2016

FEEL THE NEWNESS ARISING IN YOU

Let us dwell in the question, *what is new?*

Feel everywhere, in every instance throughout the universe, the consciousness that is sustaining and creating everything that is arising.

Enter this eternal field of pure awareness and feel the journey of your larger body, the consciousness force forming:

- Earth
- Life
- Animal life
- Human life

Bringing Earth to the bursting point of the birth of a universal humanity.

Feel your choice to enter into this incarnation, at this precise moment, at the time when your planet is calling you to express your full potential in the evolution of the world, realizing that your soul, your essence, your Evolutionary Unique Self is inspired by, and in some deep sense, remembers the whole journey of creation.

We each made a choice to be here now.

We are awakening to ourselves, as co-creators in the great Evolutionary Story of creation. The gestation is over.

The time of our birth as individual co-creators has arrived, at the exact moment when planet Earth, as a living organism, is awakening to its own birth, to its next stage of evolution.

We recognize the coinciding of our own unique expression as the impulse of evolution with the planetary birth calling for this impulse now.

We remember the choice we made.

We are asking our Unique Selves, our Evolutionary Unique Selves, to take dominion in us now.

The deepest impulse, this impulse is the Beloved, this gorgeous evolutionary impulse, is our guide. It is the Kingdom of Heaven within us. We are our own Evolutionary Unique Essential Selves.

I heard these words from my own Essential Self:

> *I will never leave you.*
>
> *I am always with you in pain, in sorrow, in misery, and in joy.*
>
> *I am now arising to consciousness in you.*

You chose to step across the threshold from the land of a separated human to the land of the connected, universal, co-creative, Unique Self.

We made the choice to step across the threshold. We are in the greatest school on Earth for the conscious evolution of humanity. There are no elders here because no one has done this before. We are one generation. We are learning.

Outrageous Love is to love one another as ourselves.

Each a unique expression of the divine impulse of creation, come into communion and community, for the birth of humanity, as co-creators with the Divine—we honor what we are doing here!

When we look outward, we see an old world dying of suffering and violence. We feel the pain of the billions and billions in the world. This pain activates our love, activates our empathy, for others. **The pain is the signal of the birth of our divine self, for the full emergence of our vocations of destiny, for the specific gift that we are to give.**

Now that we have gained evolutionary eyes, let us see the reality of what is emerging through us.

- Innovations, creative solutions, exist in every field and function.
- Innovators and creators are building new systems, new projects everywhere.
- Feel them arising from the body politic now.
- Feel them arising through each of us.

We see news of the emerging world. Feel the new arising as the news of you is arising. You step into this emerging world. You meet mentors, guides, teachers, and creators, all of us creating this new world now.

Realize each of us is a higher being, the adult universal human, the fully expressed Evolutionary Unique Self in a WeSpace during the moment of planetary evolution.

We discover each of us has the qualities of a co-creator.

Imagine our evolved universal selves drawing inward beyond our current illusion of separation. Let us join our Unique Selves, globally with everyone, everywhere, in the great communion of pioneering souls gathering, to connect for the planetary awakening in our lifetime.

DARE TO PRAY FOR NEWNESS

We are contemplatives, where still waters run deep.

We are ecstatics.

We are evangelicals.

We are bringers, together all of us, of the good news.

We are not afraid to be excited.

We are not afraid to go deep.

On this New Years. . .

>   as we are here in Bethlehem,
>   as we are here in Mecca,
>   as we are here in Beirut,
>   as we are here in Damascus,
>   as we are here in Jerusalem,
>   as we are here in Portland,
>   as we are here in Haight-Ashbury,
>   as we are here in Manhattan,
>   as we are here in the blue states and in the red states,
>   as we are here in Asia,
>   as we are here in the hinterlands of China,
>   as we are here in the islands of Japan,
>   as we are here in Malaysia,
>   as we are here in Australia,
>   as we are here in New Zealand,
>   as we come together. . .

. . . the noosphere is coming alive in us. Evolution is finding its voice, as we move from the ego of mastermind to the delight, the sensual delight that Teilhard de Chardin talked about, *when evolutionaries come together in meta-mind.*

Meta-mind is not regressive. It is progressive. Regressive, as a cult, we lose our individual voice. We lose the irreducible dignity of human rights. We lose our uniqueness.

Meta-mind is Evolutionary WeSpace, Unique Self Symphony, as the fundamental category in the new politics of Evolutionary Love, which we are going to offer to Donald Trump on Inauguration Day.

We are about to move into prayer without theme, *newness*. Newness is about new possibilities! We introduce the bare wonder of newness so we can take it into prayer because we are going to pray today for something new that we have never dared pray for before. We are going to step into a new horizon.

We are not here as a form of confirmation bias—

I am a liberal. I go to my liberal church. It confirms my liberalism.

I am an arch-conservative. I go to my conservative church. It confirms my conservatism.

No! We are about newness because evolution is about newness. Evolution is about, said Alfred North Whitehead, the creative advance of novelty. Whitehead said that evolution has three properties: the one, the many, and novelty, newness in every moment.

A little brain science, a little holy neuroscience, a little holy deep mysticism as we move into prayer: When we have to make a decision, or when we are confronted with a new situation, then our brain reviews all the situations that we previously encountered that resemble the situation. Then the brain decides what we want to do, based on the supercomputer, before we consciously think about it.

There is no newness in ordinary life. Ordinary life is about repetition. We never do anything new. The structure of neuroscience supports that.

How do you break that cycle? How do you break out of repetition?

Repetition, my friends, is depressing. But we need stability, and repetition brings stability.

The word, for example, *Rosh Hashanah*, in Hebrew is the word for New Year. The word *shana* means *shinun: the year* or *that which is repeated*.

We need repetition, right? Because we want stability.

In Hebrew, the word *shana*, year, as in New Year, means not only repetition, but it also means *shinui,* radical change, transformation, newness.

Can you imagine what it would mean to be in newness?

How do you get to that newness? What do you do?

We know in neuroscience, and we know in mysticism that there is one way to break the pattern of yesterday, to step into the new. Do you know what that is? Wonder—radical amazement—to be blown away by wonder.

Abhinavagupta, the great Kashmir Shaivite sage, he writes:

> Enlightenment is the state of continual wonder. To be enlightened is to be able to have an original moment, an original thought, an original love. Enlightenment is the realization that the moment is pregnant and birthing something that never ever was before.

Do you think this is a metaphysical idea that has nothing to do with you and me?

It has everything to do with you and me!

The only slave driver in the world, holy friends, is the belief that yesterday determines today. The only slave driver in the world is that we are limited by all of our yesterdays. It is not true!

If we enter into wonder, into radical amazement, if we enter into the deep well of silence of presence from which all creativity emerges, we can realize that the very feature of Reality is the incessant creative advance of novelty.

Not only are we physically, our cells, generating a new physical being every X amount of time. We are regenerating. We are not only becoming new physically but also mystically, interiorly, spiritually, morally, ethically, existentially; we become new.

People who are *becoming new* are how we are going to bring in a new world.

You can't remain old and create a new world.

It is why so many NGOs (non-governmental organizations) have this worldcentric consciousness. They are killing each other, fighting over territory. It is why we talk about creating a sacred vision of American politics, but behind the scenes, we are doing all sorts of crazy stuff. We can't even make peace between ourselves. No, no, no.

To become new, we have to become new. Do you get it?

That is what the Buddhists meant when they said: *You can make peace in the world when you become that peace.*

When *we* become new, when we learn *regenopause*[2], we are *becoming newer every day.*

Oh my god—is that true?

- ◆ We are becoming new every day.
- ◆ We build on the old.
- ◆ We emerge from the old.

We invite everyone to pray for something you never would have dared pray for before, to genuinely pray for newness, to pray for the impossible.

Here's a little holy secret: you want the definition of God? You can't define God. You define God, you kill God. Here is the deepest mystical understanding of God: God is the Possibility of Possibility.

---

2 *Regenopause* is a term from Barbara Marx Hubbard that she defines as: "A pause in the life cycle of the older woman when the possibility of remaking herself by choosing from her deepest impulse becomes evident."

God is the possibility of possibility to the precise extent that we are an incarnation of what Dante called, *a baby-face Divine*. We are the Possibility of Possibility.

We step into the *Hallelujah of radical newness* as we regenerate a world through regenerating ourselves.

Let's become new together. The next sangha is the Buddha. The next Buddha is the sangha. We are it! We are the ones we've been waiting for— *Hallelujah*! [*See Appendix.*]

Let us take a moment.

Let us set our intention.

Let us set it so deeply.

Here we are! We are going to get excited!

You know we are afraid to get excited. We get emails saying: *Why are we so excited? Is this evangelism?*

Yes, it is! But it is not fundamentalism.

You get it?

We are willing to get excited at a Bruce Springsteen concert. We'll spin it. We can do that. We can get excited with Jerry Garcia when we are spinning with Jerry. When Jerry is doing it, we can do it. But we are afraid to get excited for a cause. What we've done is exiled causes to fundamentalism.

So, no! We are not fundamentalists. We are not, because we are not xenophobic. We don't think that we have the one true way. We believe that all religions have great messages to the world.

We don't think you can only find it in Christ. If you are outside of Christ and you are doing Buddha, you are damned.

In all those ways, we are not fundamentalists. **But what we need to learn from fundamentalism is the ability to be excited, to bring the good news.**

Here is why Donald Trump won the election—because the liberal world stopped bringing the good news.

Postmodernism came along and said, everything is a social construction of Reality. Evolution stalled again. For the first time, the new vision of postmodernism told us what was wrong with the old vision, but didn't offer a new one.

When the new memes of consciousness do not offer a new vision in the evolution of love, consciousness moves backwards. Evolution regresses.

Donald Trump came and animated the earlier memes of consciousness.

We cannot say *we are going to exclude people who are excluded*. Of course, we don't do that. We include every victim. We include the environment which became a victim. That is not enough.

We need:

- A new vision of duty
- A new vision of honor
- A new vision of delight
- A new vision of Eros
- A new vision of sexuality
- A new vision of entrepreneurship

We need to be evangelists of genuine good news and not get upset because somebody said that Carrie Fisher was beautiful. The liberal press erupts and says, *how could Steve Martin say Carrie Fisher was beautiful?* Really, that's our cause? Let me say it here, *Carrie Fisher is beautiful.* Attack me! Are you for real? That's what the liberal press gets upset about?

- Tell me about obligation.
- Tell me about responsibility.
- Tell me about duty.

That is the excitement. There is obligation and responsibility.

What is an evolutionary ethic?

What is evolutionary integrity?

What is an *evolutionary impulse* that creates responsibility and obligation?

When we pray, we are not praying to a fundamentalist God. The God you don't believe in doesn't exist. When we pray, we affirm the dignity of personal need. We pray to the personal face of the evolutionary impulse that both lives in us and, as Rumi knew so well, holds us at the same time.

Michael Murphy, from Esalen, said about *panentheism*, which is a fancy way to say, what Rumi knew, what the mystics knew, what the Kabbalists knew: God lives in us, as us, and through us. Every place we fall, we fall into *Her* hands. Ramakrishna said: *Mother! Mother! I fall into the hands of the Mother.*

We need to reclaim prayer at a higher level of consciousness. We ask for everything. Not in obedience but in desperate plea, like children and at the same time like autonomous powerful beings—partners of God. The divine voice says: *I live in you, and I hold you, and pray to me. Ask me. Ask me for everything, and ask for something you never dared ask for before.*

Ask for everything! Dare to pray for newness!

> *I pray for the miraculous, the extraordinary, the fulfillment.*

> *May I be in every moment the living expression of love and awe and wonder. I pray that people that I've never been able to make peace with this year, I can make peace with. I pray that I can give up being right.*

Pray for other people. Pray for anyone who needs you, anyone who you can help.

> *I pray for my Uncle Morris who is having an operation. I pray for my cousin Tom who needs a heart transplant. I pray for becoming my full self. If I am only praying for myself, I am in*

*trouble. I pray for myself, and I pray for everyone. I pray for that
which I would never dare.*

For abundance to flow for all of the evolutionary projects.

For myself and for everyone to open to the newness of love.

Let the God times roll. Let the dignity of personal need roll.

Remember what Rumi said, *I'll lift you like a prayer to the sky.* With your
message, dare be charismatic! Not in the ego sense, but let the charisma
flow through you. The word is good in you, beloved whole mate. Take us to
the newness that is evolution, in this moment, alive. *Amen*!

THE SYNTHESIS OF TECHNOLOGY AND EVOLUTIONARY LOVE

Let's go into the story of what is new, to look at the growing edge of science
and technology. Let's bring the technologists in, to infuse us with their
genius, and them with our love. **If we can combine the high technology
genius in this world with the Evolutionary Love of the living presence of
the Divine, we have created a new world.**

Where is the synthesis going to take place?

A quote from Jerry Glenn, who ran the Millennium Project and has nodal
points all over the world that will be part of our Office for the Future, who
thinks there will be a new kind of civilization, one where mystics and
technologists join together.

Jerry Glenn says,

> When we merge with the mystics' attitude toward the world and
> the technologists' knowledge of the world, a new civilization
> will evolve into a continuum of technology and humanity by the
> integration of technologies within our bodies. This integration
> will be improved to the degree that mystics' and technologists'
> world views join.

When the people who have the deep inner impulse of creation alive in them—which is the technology of creation itself alive in us—are saying yes to the new technologies that are around us, they are the masters of technology. We are going to have extended bodies in every way.

We could say, to the degree that love and genius join, **one of our great purposes is to bring the greatest geniuses on Earth to join with our genius of Evolutionary Love.**

The beauty of it is that it is all here now. The new is here.

It is not just in the future.

One of the most famous people in this scientific evolutionary thought is Ray Kurzweil. Here is a quote from Ray Kurzweil:

> The first half of the 21st century, which we are now in, will be characterized by three overlapping revolutions: in genetics, in nanotechnology, and robotics. We are in the early stages of the "G" (genetic) Revolution. By understanding the information processes underlying life, we are starting to learn to reprogram our biology, to achieve the virtual elimination of disease, dramatic expansion of human potential, and radical life extension. The Nanotechnology Revolution will enable us to redesign and rebuild, molecule by molecule, bodies and brains, and the world with which we interact—going far beyond the limits of biology.

Many people are afraid of this and wish to put technology to the side. First of all, they won't be able to stop it. Secondly, it will be taken over by the military-industrial complex.

But imagine if we bring it into the heart, into the love and into the Evolutionary Story.

People in the space program are yearning for this. We might ask, *why is it that the high technology geniuses are mostly fundamentalist Christian?*

It is because they believe God is *really* at work in the world. They believe they are here to recreate a new garden, here to evolve humanity.

Kurzweil continues:

> We are going to have this ability of radical life extension. The
> end revolution will enable us to redesign and rebuild molecule
> by molecule, bodies and brains, and the world with which
> we interact, going far beyond the limits of biology. The most
> powerful impending revolution is the R or human-level robots
> with their intelligence derived from our own, but redesigned to
> far exceed human capacities. R represents the most significant
> transformation because intelligence is the most powerful force
> in the universe. Intelligence, if sufficiently advanced, is smart
> enough to overcome any obstacle in its way.

Nanotechnology stands for building, atom by atom by atom, the way nature
does. One of the young men who invented nanotechnology said: *I think we
can do resurrection from the dead. We could take the simplest cell, and it can
be resurrected because it is a DNA. It is an information code.*

We are a manifestation of information-coding, so this is now possible.

What are we going to do about this? We have to open our minds and our
hearts to this.

Who is going to guide this intelligence?

Shall we turn it over to the current political, military, industrial system
where it is at? Or, **shall we bring the technologists home to the impulse
of evolution within them?**

Ray Kurzweil goes further to say:

> We are hitting a singularity. A future period during which the
> pace of technological change will be so rapid, its impact so deep,
> that human life will be irreversibly transformed by The Law of
> Accelerating Returns. Inherent acceleration of rate of evolution
> with technological evolution as a continuum of biological
> evolution.

So, when we say *The Universe: A Love Story*—connecting particles to particles through allurement, all the way up and all the way down—is it not true that this is the very same process of joining genius at the level of the technological skills with the love and the impulse of evolution toward higher consciousness, freedom, and order? Do you see the incredible possibility?

Ray Kurzweil again:

> The key idea underlying the impending singularity is that the pace of change of our human-created technology is accelerating, and its powers are expanding at an exponential rate. This will represent the merger of our biological thinking and existence with technology, resulting in a world that is still human but transcends our biological roots. There will be no distinction post-singularity between human, machine, and virtual reality. Matter and mechanisms of the universe will be transformed into exquisitely sublime forms of intelligence.

Saint Paul said, *Behold, I show you a mystery. We shall not all sleep, we shall all be changed.*

Jesus said, *You will do the work that I did, and greater works than these will you do in the fullness of time.*

Do you think that this is exactly the fullness of time and these powers now have to be brought into love?

We are completely getting over the idea that we are the final result of evolution and it stops here with *Homo sapiens sapiens* and self-centered consciousness.

James Gardner said:

> We are entering the Virtual Cambrian Age. Approximately half a billion years ago, a flash of the evolutionary eye, life crossed a portentous threshold, a fleeting instant. In geological terms, a wild profusion of animal body parts appeared—head, neck,

arms, legs.

They weren't there before, but they seemed to be a good idea. Many creatures have heads, arms, legs, and so forth.

In the late 20th century, the forces of cultural evolution crossed a threshold. We acquired technological capacity to intervene directly in the redesign of the human genome, as well as build technological extensions of human capability. I call this a new evolutionary watershed, the Virtual Cambrian Age.

Not only are we going to radically extend our life, but let's take this computer that we are on, looking at each other from around the world, talking at each other, this is an extension in the post-Cambrian age of our body-minds.

We take this extension as a gift from God.

We take our cellphones as an extension of our global brain.

We are saying *Yes* to the extended capacities of humanity—if filled with love.

Bruce Lipton has a book called *Spontaneous Evolution*. He states, *The field is the sole governing agency of the particle. The material universe is shaped by the invisible field, the matrix.*

We are generating the field. Genes are blueprints, not destiny. They are triggered on and off by environment and perception.

Bruce Lipton continues, *a new revolutionary field in biology is called epigenetics, control above genetics, reveals that genes are not destiny.*

This is Mark Cummings. This is about zero-point. This is our favorite. Mark Cummings writes:

> The fact is that by many estimates, there abides in one cubic centimeter of empty space, an amount of energy greater than the total amount of energy contained or expressed in all the matter of the known universe. This energy is called zero-point energy. Because it was discovered that even at or around absolute zero,

which is, by definition, the temperature where all thermal motion is supposed to cease, there was and still is irreducible motion, which was clearly non-thermal in nature.

Here is the key line:

We are immersed in a field of infinite energy density, in the guise of what appears to be empty space. Space is a highly potentiated, energetic medium, shining with vast luminous force, and shimmering with intrinsic sentience. Solid footing to a fundamentally abundance-based worldview, a much needed antidote to the scourge of nihilistic materialism.

What is new is what comes through spirit technology. Let's be fierce in our willingness to become new: we are the possibility of possibility.

INTERIORS AND EXTERIORS ARE ONE

The words are one. There are no obstacles. All obstacles are melted away. The word is good.

Let us feel into this. What have we done?

Ray Kurzweil makes such a huge contribution. Let's hold his beautiful truth, but his truth is *true but partial.* Kurzweil externalized transformation. He externalized newness to the technological world.

His cousin, Arthur, is also a great thinker. Arthur Kurzweil is a great publisher of books, the editor-in-chief of Jason Aronson.

Do you see what happened? **The evolution of new visions of love, the evolution of new visions of obligation, the evolution of interiority, the evolution of God has, in some sense, *stalled.***

Back in the sixteenth century—can you imagine if you went to a doctor today, and the doctor said, *let me do a little bloodletting, let me put some leeches on you, and I'll charge your health insurance.* Oh my god! You would file for malpractice insurance in one second. We don't allow medicine to be four centuries old because it has to be new.

Somehow, our vision of Spirit is four centuries old for most people, which means God is not evolving. We have exiled evolution to technology.

What we are now saying is:

- Interiors and exteriors are one.
- There is no split between the animate, the inside and the outside, the animate and the inanimate.
- It is sentience all the way up and all the way down.

We need a power of interiors commensurate to the power of exteriors. We need a newness to transform our very cells, but that is not going to happen merely through technology. Transformation will happen through interior and exterior technology meeting in the bliss of the eschaton.

We need a newness on the inside commensurate with the newness on the outside.

I want to give us a simple practice. There was a great master, Israel of Salanter, and he said:

> When I was young, I wanted to make the whole world new. I wanted to change the whole world. When I got older, the whole world was too much. I'll change my country. I got a little older, that was too much. I'm going to change to make my city new, that was too much. I got a little older, he said, maybe my neighborhood and my family. He said now, I just want to do one new thing, I want to change one thing in myself before I pass.

Newness begins with my own transformation.

Newness means:
- Am I willing to call someone today that I've been in a clash with for twenty years?
- Am I willing to give up being right?

- ◆ Am I willing to reach out to people who I've let go?
- ◆ Am I willing to call my mother who I haven't called for seven years?
- ◆ Am I willing to reach out to an estranged partner, who had changed the locks on the house and sued and I am locked in an argument with?
- ◆ Will I let newness, a new heart, a new heaven, a new Earth, enter in?

The only way we are going to create a new world and create a singularity equal to our power and equal to our love is if we become new.

The cellphone, which is an extension of our body, has to be invested with love, with Outrageous Love. Not ordinary love. Ordinary love, remember, is a strategy of ego.

Outrageous Love is the love that is the heart of existence itself, that loves every moment open into a new possibility.

The only heresy in the entire world is that there is an extra person and an extra moment. There is no extra person.

No one is extra on the set. There is no extra moment.

Every moment is here to birth something, undeniably new.

God is the possibility of possibility. God is an Outrageous Lover. It is Outrageous Love that births Reality into existence.

We live in a world of outrageous pain. The only response to outrageous pain is Outrageous Love. That is the sutra.

As divine miniatures, as participants in Divine, as the new Christ, we are the possibility of possibility.

If you think you can talk about newness from today till tomorrow, and you can write about newness, if we think we can talk about newness, but not become new ourselves, *we are full of shit.*

Becoming new means:

- Finding the place that is hard.
- Forgiving who you do not want to forgive.
- Stepping into a possibility for your life that you are afraid of because you are afraid of your greatness.

We need your greatness!

Reality needs your greatness!

When a person gets married in the mystical Hebrew tradition, called the Day of Atonement, you fast on that day and you forgive everyone before you get married.

You know why? Because, if you hate one person in your heart, you can't create. If you hate another person in your heart, then you shut down another part of yourself. Let go of our hatreds. Do not be naive, tie our camel to a post, but:

- Let's be fierce in our love.
- Let's be fierce in our willingness to become new.
- Let's be fierce in the possibility of possibility.
- Let's be fierce in our commitments.
- Let's be fierce in forgiveness.

The people we need to sit with and make it new are the people that we think it is impossible to sit with. **Be willing to sit with anyone in the world, anywhere in the world, no exceptions, and make it new.** Be willing to give up being right about anything.

Check the facts.

Check the evidence.

Check the information.

Check it all together.

Let's all give up being right together.

Let's commit to our holy partners all the way

Let's be whole mates all the way in this lifetime.

Let's create a new Reality.

Let's create heaven on Earth.

This is the time, the possibility of possibility.

We are the ones we've been waiting for.

God needs our service. God is waiting for us.

APPENDIX: SONGS

THE BATTLE HYMN OF THE REPUBLIC—JULIA WARD HOWE[3]

Mine eyes have seen the glory of the coming of the Lord.

He has trampled down the vintage
   where the grapes of wrath are stored.

He has loosed the fateful lightning
   of his terrible swift sword.

His truth is marching on.

HOW COULD ANYONE—LIBBY RODERICK[4]

How could anyone ever tell you
   you were anything less than beautiful?

How could anyone ever tell you
   you were less than whole?

How could anyone fail to notice
   that your loving is a miracle—
   how deeply you're connected to my soul?

---

3   Julia Ward Howe, "The Battle Hymn of the Republic," 1862.

4   Libby Roderick, "How Could Anyone," on *If You See a Dream* (Turtle Island Records, 1990), CD.

I WANT TO KNOW WHAT LOVE IS—FOREIGNER[5]

I've gotta take a little time,
a little time to think things over.
I better read between the lines,
in case I need it when I'm older.
(Whoa, ooh-ooh, ooh-ooh)

And this mountain, I must climb
feels like the world upon my shoulders,
and through the clouds, I see love shine,
it keeps me warm as life grows colder.

[Pre-Chorus]
In my life, there's been heartache and pain.
I don't know if I can face it again.
Can't stop now, I've travelled so far
to change this lonely life.

[Chorus]
I wanna know what love is.
I want you to show me.
I wanna feel what love is.
I know you can show me.
Oh, oh-oh, oh (ooh)

I'm gonna take a little time,
a little time to look around me.
I've got nowhere left to hide,
it looks like love has finally found me.

[Pre-Chorus]

[Chorus]

[Outro]

(And I wanna feel) I wanna feel what love is

---

5   Foreigner, "I Want To Know What Love Is," recorded November 1984, on *Agent Provocateur*, Atlantic Records, vinyl LP.

(And I know) I know you can show me.
Let's talk about love.
(I wanna know what love is) The love that you feel inside.
(I want you to show me) And I'm feelin' so much love.
(I wanna feel what love is) No, you just cannot hide.
(I know you can show me) Yeah.
I wanna know what love is (Let's talk about love).
I want you to show me, I wanna feel.
(I wanna feel what love is) And I know, and I know.
I know you can show me (Yeah).
(I wanna know what love is) (I wanna know)
(I want you to show me) I wanna know, I wanna know, wanna know.
(I wanna feel what love is) (I wanna feel)
(I know you can show me).

HALLELUJAH—LEONARD COHEN[6]

Now, I've heard there was a secret chord
that David played, and it pleased the Lord.
But you don't really care for music, do you?
It goes like this, the fourth, the fifth,
the minor fall, the major lift.
The baffled king composing Hallelujah.

[Chorus]

Hallelujah, Hallelujah,
Hallelujah, Hallelujah.

Your faith was strong, but you needed proof.
You saw her bathing on the roof.
Her beauty and the moonlight overthrew you.
She tied you to a kitchen chair,
she broke your throne, and she cut your hair,
and from your lips she drew the Hallelujah.

---

6 Leonard Cohen, "Hallelujah", Various Positions, Columbia Records, 1984, LP.

[Chorus]

You say I took the name in vain,
I don't even know the name,
but if I did, well, really, what's it to you?
There's a blaze of light in every word,
it doesn't matter which you heard,
the holy or the broken Hallelujah.

[Chorus]

I did my best, it wasn't much.
I couldn't feel, so I tried to touch.
I've told the truth, I didn't come to fool you.
And even though it all went wrong,
I'll stand before the Lord of Song
With nothing on my tongue but Hallelujah.

OM NAMAH SHIVAAYA

Om Namah Shivaaya
Shivaaya namaha,
Shivaaya namah om
Shivaaya namaha, namaha Shivaaya
Shambhu Shankara namah Shivaaya,
Girijaa Shankara namah Shivaaya
Arunaachala Shiva namah Shivaaya

*I bow to the soul of all. I bow to my Self. I don't know who I am,
so I bow to you, Shiva, my own true Self. I bow to my teachers
who loved me with love. Who took care of me when I couldn't
take care of myself. I owe everything to them. How can I repay
them? They have everything in the world. Only my love is mine
to give, but in giving I find that it is their love flowing through
me back to the world...I have nothing. I have everything. I want
nothing. Only let it flow to you, my love... sing!*

INDEX

Volume 1 — A Planetary Awakening in Love Through Unique Self Symphonies

LIST OF EPISODES

1. Episode 1 — October 29, 2016

2. Episode 2 — November 5, 2016

3. Episode 3 — November 12, 2016

4. Episode 4 — November 19, 2016

5. Episode 5 — December 3, 2016

6. Episode 6 — December 10, 2016

7. Episode 7 — December 17, 2016

8. Episode 8 — December 24, 2016

9. Episode 9 — December 31, 2016

www.ingramcontent.com/pod-product-compliance
Lightning Source LLC
LaVergne TN
LVHW011154080426
835508LV00007B/407